UNITED STATES I

MW01092677

BUREAU OF LAND MANAGEMENT

Most of the Mojave Road Recreation Trail is on the public lands administered by the Bureau of Land Management. BLM was involved in development of this trail and fully approves of its use. BLM believes travel along the Mojave Road will be greatly enhanced through use of the Mojave Road Guide. Without the Guide the Mojave Road is just another rough road, of which there are hundreds in the desert. With the Guide the Mojave Road becomes a classroom on wheels and the traveler is in for an entirely different kind of experience. BLM maintains a supply of Guides for sale to the public and as loaners to those who do not wish to purchase them. Contact any of the offices indicated below. Remember at all times, that our freedom for continued use of the back roads of the desert under multiple-use concepts, depends entirely upon full cooperation with BLM. Do not hesitate to contact them with any matter concerning management of these key public lands.

California Desert District
1695 Spruce Street
Riverside, CA 92507
(714) 351-6394

Needles Resource Area
901 Third Street
Needles, CA 92363
(619) 326-3896

U. S. DEPARTMENT OF THE INTERIOR
BUREAU OF LAND MANAGEMENT

Las Vegas District Office
4765 Vegas Drive
Las Vegas, NV 89126
(702) 388-6403

Barstow Resource Area
831 Barstow Road
Barstow, CA 92311
(619) 256-3591

MOJAVE ROAD GUIDE

TED JENSEN

MOJAVE ROAD GUIDE

by

Dennis G. Casebier

and the

Friends of the Mojave Road

Tales of the Mojave Road

Number 11

June 1986

Tales of the Mojave Road
Publishing Company
P.O. Box 307
Norco, California 91760

Dennis G. Casebier
Goffs School House
HCR G No. 15
Essex, CA 92332

Copyright © by Dennis G. Casebier 1986

Library of Congress Catalog Card Number
86-50396

ISBN 0-914224-13-1

Printing by
The A-to-Z Printing Company
of
Riverside, California

Binding by
National Bindery Company
of
Pomona, California

WARNING

WARNING

Important Notice

This Guide to the Mojave Road is <u>not</u> designed to serve as a survival manual. Desert travel always presents a risk of danger to life and property. Nobody can anticipate the full spectrum of difficulties that can be encountered by the desert traveler and absolutely no effort has been made to do that in this Guide. The next emergency that occurs on the desert will be something that is totally unanticipated by the participants, the Friends of the Mojave Road, the Bureau of Land Management, or anyone else. Therefore, those who choose to travel in the desert, whether it be on the Mojave Road or elsewhere, do so at their own risk.

WARNING

CONTENTS

MAPS

MOJAVE INDIANS

Mojave Indians as they appeared to the Whipple Railroad Survey party in 1854. From: REPORTS OF EXPLORATIONS AND SURVEYS, TO ASCERTAIN THE MOST PRACTICABLE AND ECONOMICAL ROUTE FOR A RAILROAD FROM THE MISSISSIPPI RIVER TO THE PACIFIC OCEAN (Vol III), by Lt. Amiel Weeks Whipple and others.

Drawing by Henrich Baldwin Mollhausen

INTRODUCTION

The historical importance of the Mojave Road has been well established in the literature of the California Deserts. Over the past 20 years a growing number of people have become familiar with the significant role the Mojave Road played in the years 1860-1880 and even earlier. In recent years the trail itself has been gaining attention for its educational and recreational use.

In May of 1981 interest in developing the recreational potential of the trail was formalized with creation of a group called Friends of the Mojave Road. At that time the mailing list of the Friends amounted to only about 25 people. Now there are over 1,500 names on the list and the number continues to grow.

Since May of 1981 the Friends of the Mojave Road have labored to transform the Mojave Road into a recreation trail. Through the efforts of these volunteers, the trail has been marked out on the ground, careful maps have been drawn, thousands of photographs have been taken, and finally, in November of 1983, the first edition of this Guide was published.

The story of the reopening of the Mojave Road as a recreation trail is long, complicated, and (we hope) interesting. That story has been written as a book by itself and hence the story is available in detail. That precludes the need to say much more here about the struggle that led to the establishment of the Mojave Road as a recreation trail.

Since publication of the original Guide more than 2,000 people have passed over the Mojave Road. The reactions they have recorded at the Mail Box at Mile 74.3 and our observations of the condition of the road itself after that much use, convinces us that we have indeed developed a nondestructive way to make educational and recreational use of the desert. This has led to our determination to keep the Guide in print and available to an expanding and interested public.

We produced about 1,700 copies of the original GUIDE TO THE MOJAVE ROAD. It is out of print and demand continues. There have been pressures for a shortened and less expensive version. Also, some changes have taken place in the country through which the Mojave Road passes suggesting the appropriateness of a revision to the Guide. These factors have given rise to this revised edition of the GUIDE TO THE MOJAVE ROAD. We hope those of you who purchase and

9.

use it will find the Mojave Road experience to be as enjoyable and uplifting as the people who went before you.

Literally hundreds of people have assisted in the Mojave Road Project. It is not possible to mention them all. I freely acknowledge that the Mojave Road Recreation Trail would not have been possible without them.

The direct effort involved in production of a book of this kind is enormous. I find myself frequently telling my friends (usually in response to questions like "Why can't you go this weekend?") that unless you've put a book like this together you just can't understand the amount of work involved.

I received much valued direct assistance in production of the book. Without that assistance it wouldn't have gotten done. Mel Bogle made photo reductions on all the D. Ratt cartoons. Neal Johns read early versions of the manuscript, checked mileages, and made many suggestions for improvements. Spence Murray read the manuscript for typos and other corrections several times. Jo Ann Smith read the manuscript and typeset copies many times and performed plethora of other support chores in preparation for publication. Bob Martin made all the maps that appear in the book. Millie Hinsvark did some of the typographic artwork. Irv Dierdorff and Mike Marino have assisted in the photographic department. Marlou Casebier read the typeset copies, assisted with layout and preparation of picture captions, and performed many other tasks. Pat Davison, Dick MacPherson, and Linda and Gary Overson assisted with the cartoon captions for the desert awareness section. Dick MacPherson also worked in rechecking some of the mileages and routes in the field and he contributed photographs. Many thanks to you all and I'll repeat -- It wouldn't have happened without your help!

Dennis G. Casebier
Corona, California

July 4, 1986

GENERAL GUIDELINES

There are no signs telling you where to go anywhere on the Mojave Road throughout the 138.8 miles from the Colorado River to Camp Cady. You must rely on maps (including these in this book), the descriptive narrative in this book, and the rock cairns placed along the way.

When you are traveling the trail from the Colorado River toward Camp Cady, the cairns will always be on your right. Generally this means they are on the north side of the road. Of course there are places where the road twists and turns and heads toward the north or south, although the general direction is east and west. The rule is that the cairns will always be on the right side when you are headed toward Los Angeles.

The cairns are about two feet high, although there is considerable variation in size. In some cases there may be just a few stones piled up. In at least one case (east side of Watson Wash), the cairn was built to be waist high so it would be visible from the Cedar Canyon Road.

In areas where there was loose rock in the immediate vicinity of the road, then that rock was used, and hence the cairns blend in with the background and may be difficult to see. Along rockless stretches stones were hauled in to build the cairns and frequently these stand out better. In many places, the cairns have been there long enough that they have been partly or totally obscured by desert plants.

The rocks have a tendency to tumble off the cairns. This might be caused by people, cattle, wind, earth tremors, faulty construction, or a combination of things. When you see that this has happened, you may want to stack the rocks back up or do whatever rebuilding seems to be required. It will help the next traveler.

The basic policy was to put cairns at every intersection with other roads (however faint these roads may be), at major washes where the road might be difficult to follow after floods, and at other places as it was deemed necessary or convenient. There was no effort to put cairns at regular intervals, but where the way is confusing we put them close together. Frequently in these instances one cairn will be in sight of the next one.

But you are not left with the cairns alone to guide you over the trail. Equally important is the set of specially drawn maps. These include one small-scale map that covers the entire East Mojave and which is the key to the other large-scale maps. Generally speaking, the small-scale map is used to find the Mojave Road from modern roads while the large-scale maps are used to follow the Mojave Road after you get on it.

The most important feature on the large-scale maps is the mileage numbers. There are two sets of numbers. The series on the left side of the page start with Mile 0.0 at the Colorado River and run continuously to Mile 138.8 at Camp Cady. The mileages at the end of each entry give you the distance to the next described feature.

There are no mileage indicators on the ground or along the trail; they appear only on the maps. Refer to these mileages for the narrative directions necessary to enable you to follow the trail on the ground. Descriptions of history and other subjects of interest are also keyed to these mileages.

The plan is that you will watch the maps as you go along, simultaneously reading the narrative that goes with the country you're passing through, and all the while watching for cairns as a check that you're on the right track.

The mileages along the trail are as accurate as we could measure them and make them fit the maps. You cannot expect your own odometer readings to agree exactly. The mileages are useful to tell you where you are within normal odometer accuracy, so you'll know about how far it is to the various landmarks.

VEHICLE AND OTHER REQUIREMENTS
MISCELLANEOUS WARNINGS

Most of the country traversed by the Mojave Road is desert wilderness, although it is not officially designated as "wilderness" in the technical sense. It is far removed from civilization. Days may pass without seeing anyone. The distances to services are great. It is a place of remarkable beauty and solitude, and yet it can be a place of great danger if something goes wrong and the traveler finds himself short on equipment or knowledge of what to do. THIS GUIDE IS NOT A SURVIVAL BOOK. If you are inexperienced in desert travel or if your knowledge of what equipment you should have or what to do in emergencies is lacking, then don't expect this book to correct these deficiencies. You must get your knowledge of desert survival elsewhere.

If you are going to travel the Mojave Road, the following constraints should guide your plans and equipment selections.

***There must be more than one vehicle in the group.

***All vehicles must have four-wheel drive.

***Have sufficient gasoline to go 150 miles in 4WD.

***Carry sufficient emergency food and water to last a week.

***Know what you are going to do in case of snake bite or other serious injury.

***File a travel plan with officials or friends.

***Check the status of Soda Lake before attempting a crossing. If there has been a recent rain or the Mojave River has flooded recently, go around by way of Baker; if in doubt, don't attempt a crossing.

***As you travel the trail, develop the policy that each vehicle is responsible for keeping the vehicle behind him in sight. If necessary, wait at each turn or cross-road for the vehicle behind you to appear.

***All vehicles should have snatch ropes, tow chains, or similar devices. It is advisable to have at least one with a winch.

***Leave considerable space between vehicles crossing Soda Lake, so only one vehicle gets stuck in case of mud. The same advice applies to the sandy areas of the Mojave River Floodplain east of Afton Canyon.

***The bed of the Mojave River west of Afton Canyon can be extremely sandy. Inexperienced drivers, even with 4WD, can get stuck. Many off-road drivers let some of the air out of their tires for better floatation in sand. Check with your tire expert before doing this for a proper procedure with your tires.

***If you plan to go from the Colorado River to Camp Cady, or Manix Wash, you'll need at least two full days; a minimum of three days is recommended.

13.

***It can be extremely hot in the low country in summer. Many people choose to stay above 3,000 feet from June to September. And remember, it can snow in the high country in winter. There will even be rare occasions when heavy snow is encountered after winter storms, especially in Round Valley. Be prepared for very cold nights in winter months. Weather-wise, the best months to travel the Mojave Road are October and November and March and April -- but, of course, some experienced people enjoy it the year around.

***The firmness of sand varies significantly depending upon how moist it is. If it has rained within a month or two of when you pass through a sandy area, and if the weather has not been hot and winds have not been strong, the sand may be firm. Later in the year, after it has been hot and much time has passed without rain, the road that was so easy and firm before may now be a trap of soft powdery sand. Watch for it. Proceed cautiously into areas where sand has drifted. Leave considerable space between vehicles so only one gets stuck if you hit unexpectedly bad sand.

***"Never camp in washes or stream beds in desert country" is a wise rule to follow. Flash floods of unbelievable intensity can appear without warning.

DESERT ETIQUETTE

A tour of the Mojave Road should be a positive and socially uplifting experience. If the traveler opens his mind to the desert, to the narrative in this Guide, and to the reality of the desert around him, then he'll emerge from traveling over the trail better informed about the natural and human history of the desert and with a frame of mind more optimistic and positive.

This off-road vehicle experience is not a contest or challenge with the land or with other travelers. The challenge to the vehicle user is to experience the natural wonders of a harsh desert region, which was overcome by the pioneers and founders of the Mojave Road. Satisfy yourself that your style of use will not result in damage to the environment, to your vehicle, or to yourself.

The freedom with which we are permitted to travel through this desert country, together with its great natural beauty, including scenery, flora, and fauna, are the essential and fundamental values of this experience. These values are perishable. Never has the admonishment "abuse it and you'll lose it" had more direct application. It is a fact that this public land belongs to you and me, but we do not have the right to use it in any way that damages its essential values.

Nobody will be looking over your shoulder. You are free to behave however you wish. But we believe the following basic ideas of behavior should be followed to guarantee that we all will continue to be free to pursue this experience, and to preserve and protect the vital elements of the desert's perishable resources.

Put yourself for a moment in the position of the cattle ranchers. Be respectful of them and their property. Be friendly to them, and they will be friendly back. Be understanding if they act a little suspicious. They have reason to be concerned. Their livelihood is out there wandering around virtually unprotected. We mention the cattle industry specifically because the road passes through so much cattle country and because their property is so exposed. The same advice applies to other desert users you might meet.

Stay on the road, except to park or camp. Scenic quality is an essential part of this experience. Random vehicle tracks in the wilderness will spoil it.

Take all your trash home. If the other fellow has been more careless, help us all out. Take his trash home too. Remember, if you haul it in, haul it out.

Bring your own firewood. The desert does not offer enough. Gathering dead and down wood is allowed at the present time (free use -- no permit required) for use in the desert, but cutting of live wood is not permitted anywhere.

Bring all the guns you want, but please don't discharge them during your Mojave Road experience. The noise has a negative impact on the outing. Don't kill anything unnecessarily, even a Mojave Green Rattlesnake. This is not a killing experience. "Live and let live" as you pass over the Mojave Road. Go shoot somewhere else, some other time.

Most damage to historical and archeological sites on the desert comes in tiny increments. Ordinary people, with no malice of forethought, sometimes do little things they think don't matter. Say, they take a stone from a wall. Perhaps the stone is taken home as a souvenir. In time it loses its identify and becomes just another rock. But back on the desert it was a vital part of a historical structure that people enjoyed seeing. Then others come along and do the same thing. The accumulated effect is major. With the increasing number of visitors now, a historical structure can be devastated in a short time. Please leave everything for the next fellow to enjoy, just as you did. Take home your pictures; take home your memories; and take home the feeling that, as far as you are concerned, everything will be the same when you go back again.

In a few places the Mojave Road passes through areas where there is unmarked private land. BLM has an active program to acquire legal easements in these cases. Meanwhile, be advised that this Guide does not provide data to tell you when you are in the vicinity of private land. BLM publishes land status maps that can be used for this. There could be nervousness about increased traffic on the Mojave Road by landowners adjacent to it. Our objective is to allay their concerns through our good citizenship. Of course each of us is personally responsible to behave lawfully and with courtesy with respect to private property of all kinds that might be encountered on the desert.

Be very careful of the wildlife on the desert. It is a harsh land and some of the denizens of the desert have a harsh appearance. But be mindful of how rare they are and what a thrill it is to see them. Stand back and observe them and leave them undisturbed as you pass over the Mojave Road.

The Mojave Road would not have been developed without support and interest by BLM officials. The road is mostly on public land. They are responsible for it. They are your agents in this matter, and they approve of the use you're making of the desert. If you travel the Mojave Road, drop the BLM people in Needles, Riverside, or Barstow a line and give them your views on this use of the desert. They need to know the public is using it, and they need to know what aspects of the experience you benefitted from or enjoyed the most. Also, it would help if you report to BLM any irregularities or problems you've observed while driving the Mojave Road.

Dennis G. Casebier
Chairman
Friends of the Mojave Road

July 4, 1986

VARIATIONS IN ELEVATION ALONG THE TRAIL

The significant changes in elevation experienced as you pass over the Mojave Road is one of the major features of the trail. At Mile 0.0 you are at an elevation of less than 500 feet. In Round Valley in the Mid Hills Region you are over 5,000 feet. This change takes you through the entire spectrum of Mojave Desert flora and fauna because rainfall is heavier and temperatures are cooler at the higher elevations, and hence there is more vegetation at higher elevations. Keep in mind that it can be extremely cold (snow is not uncommon) at high elevations in the winter and extremely hot (dangerously hot!) at low elevations in the summer. Following is a list of selected elevations at key points along the Mojave Road Recreation Trail.

Mile	Point on the Trail	Elevation (feet)
0.0	Colorado River	490
11.1	Forks of the Road	2,640
14.3	Intersection with U.S. Highway 95	2,260
23.5	Fort Piute	2,800
31.4	Top of Piute Mountain	3,580
41.9	Intersection with Ivanpah-Goffs Road	4,080
50.5	Rock Spring	4,800
52.6	Government Holes	5,040
54.8	Head of Cedar Canyon (high point)	5,167
62.6	Intersection with Kelso-Cima Road	3,725
70.8	Marl Springs	3,900
74.3	Mail Box	4,320
79.2	Intersection -- Aiken Cinder Mine Road	3,190
85.8	Intersection with Kelbaker Road	2,200
88.0	Seventeenmile Point	2,000
96.7	Volunteer Gate	940
97.1	to 102.4 -- Crossing Soda Lake	930
102.4	The Granites	930
104.5	Intersection with Rasor Road	1,020
106.7	Shaw Pass	1,170
108.4	Eastern Edge of Floodplain	1,080
114.0	Intersection with Basin Road	1,190
120.0	The Caves in Afton Canyon	1,360
121.4	BLM Afton Canyon Campground	1,440
128.9	Intersection with Field Road	1,540
129.7	The Triangles	1,590
134.0	Intersection with Manix Wash Road	1,630
138.8	Camp Cady	1,680

EXPLANATION OF THE MAPS

The Mojave Road Recreation Trail runs from the east (in southern Nevada on the Colorado River opposite Fort Mojave) to the west (Camp Cady) along the line marked with stars on this large map of the East Mojave Desert. The small rectangles show the location of the detailed maps that are reproduced on the indicated pages in this Guide. The narrative in the book is arranged by mileage along the road, beginning at Mile 0.0 on the Colorado River, and ending 138.8 miles to the west at Camp Cady. The detailed maps are sandwiched in with this text so that each map precedes the section of narrative with which it is associated. The following are the symbols used on the detailed maps.

LEGEND FOR DETAILED MAPS

================ Mojave Road Recreation Trail.

·················· Hiking Trails.

— — — — — Dirt/Jeep Roads.

=-=-=-= Graded Dirt Roads.

━━━━━ Paved Roads.

+++++++ Railroads.

—/—/—/— High Lines (Power Transmission Lines).

—x—x—x— Fence Lines.

— ·· — ·· — Boundary Lines.

Washes (usually dry).

Lava Bed Edges.

Restricted Area.

△ Points of Interest.

0	1	2	3	4

Scale -- Miles

MOJAVE INDIANS

"Dwellings of the Natives of the Rio Colorado of the West." A scene in Mojave Valley drawn by artist Henrich Baldwin Mollhausen who visited the valley with Whipple in 1854. From: DIARY OF A JOURNEY FROM THE MISSISSIPPI TO THE COASTS OF THE PACIFIC WITH THE UNITED STATES GOVERNMENT EXPEDITION (Vol. II), by Baldwin Mollhausen.

FORT MOJAVE, ARIZONA TERRITORY
The picture was taken at Fort Mojave in 1871 by Timothy O. O'Sullivan, photographer with the Wheeler Expedition. O'Sullivan was standing on a roof with the Colorado River to his back. This view is taken to the southeast and shows the officers' quarters.

National Archives Collections

MOJAVE ROAD GUIDE

GETTING TO MILE 0.0
FROM NEEDLES, CALIFORNIA

Of course users of the Mojave Road are free to travel it in either direction, travel segments of it, visit just certain of the sites along the way, or make use of whatever approach best suits them and satisfies their personal interests. Many of our caravan treks over the Mojave Road have been structured by traveling to Needles the night before the trek is to start, stay in a motel there (or camp in the desert north of there at some point convenient to the trail head), and commence the trek over the trail the next day. This approach has been used many times and it works well. So, for our present purposes, we'll assume the traveler is in Needles and is positioned on River Road on the bridge over I-40 headed north. It is a little tricky to find the Mojave Road from River Road, partly because the main road becomes Pew Road about 5.5 miles north of Needles. In any case, until you reach the turnoff to the Mojave Road, stay on the main blacktopped road headed north toward Laughlin, Nevada.

Mile 0.0. On River Road on bridge over I-40 in Needles. (0.6).

Mile 0.6. Bear right at the "Y" and continue on River Road. (5.0).

Mile 5.6. Bear left at the "Y". You are now on Pew Road heading toward the Dead Mountains and on the highway to Laughlin, NV. (1.3).

Mile 6.9. Pew Road is now heading directly north. (5.5).

Mile 12.4. On the right is a sign saying "Von Schmidt Historical Marker." (0.1).

Mile 12.5. Von Schmidt marker on right. Stop and read the plaque if you have time. See discussion of this monument at Mile 3.0 on the Mojave Road Log. (2.6).

19.

FORT MOJAVE INDIAN SCHOOL

This photograph was taken in the 1920s on the west bank of the Colorado River looking east across the river at the Fort Mojave Indian School. The picture is unusual in that most of the many photographs of Fort Mojave and the Fort Mojave Indian School were taken at the site on the east bank. Fortunately for us, this photographer stood exactly at Mile 0.0 on the future Mojave Road Recreation Trail to take this historic shot.

Betty Ordway Collection

FORT MOJAVE INDIAN SCHOOL
"Students" at the Fort Mojave Indian School lined up for inspection in about 1902. The picture was taken by Minnie Braithwaite Jenkins, a teacher at the school at that time. The view is to the west. The mountains in the distance are the Dead Mountains. The dip in the horizon in the left part of the picture marks the location of Picture Canyon.
Dorothy Jenkins Ross Collection

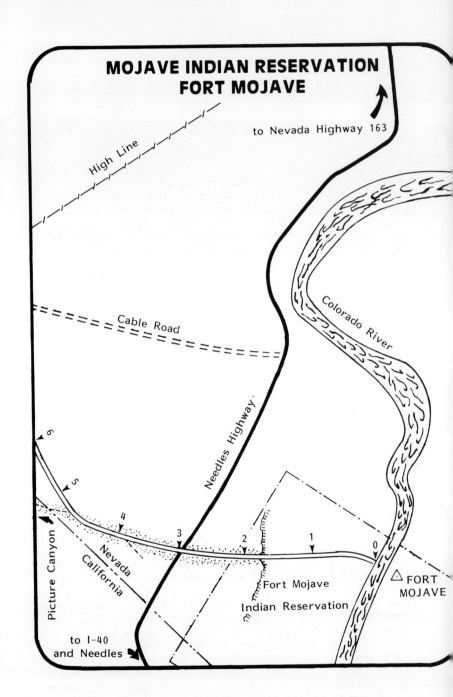

MOJAVE INDIAN RESERVATION
FORT MOJAVE

to Nevada Highway 163

High Line

Cable Road

Colorado River

Needles Highway

6

5

4

3

2

1

0

Picture Canyon

Nevada

California

Fort Mojave

Indian Reservation

△ FORT MOJAVE

to I-40
and Needles

22.

Mile 15.1. There is a Nevada boundary sign on the right that says "Welcome to Nevada, the Silver State, Clark County." (0.3).

Mile 15.4. A "Do Not Pass" sign on the right. (0.45).

Mile 15.85. Mojave Road crosses here, turn right toward the river.

You are at Mile 3.0 on the Mojave Road at this point so it is exactly three miles to the edge of the river, which is Mile 0.0. Drive to the river to begin your trip on the Mojave Road Recreation Trail. The river bottom here is on the Fort Mojave Indian Reservation and so the Indians have the right to control access.

0   You are on the west bank of the Colorado River. Now the Colorado is only a narrow channel here, where once, before the building of the great dams upstream, it was one of the great rivers of the world. The amount of water flowing through the river bed now is controlled. In the past, when the river was in its natural state, there were times, usually in winter, when the flow dwindled to an insignificant amount. There were other times, in June or early July, as the snow was melting in the Rocky Mountains, when it was a raging torrent more than a mile wide.

This spot is in the heart of what was once the great Mojave Indian Nation. Today it is part of the Fort Mojave Indian Reservation. When the white man first came here, it was an important location in the midst of a nation of about 2,500 Mojave Indians that stretched from the Needles on the south to Bullhead Rock on the north. Since they were agricultural Indians, they had spare time and were inveterate travelers. Their route to the Pacific, which they used extensively to exchange their food products for sea shells, is what became the Mojave Road. The quantity of goods carried over the trail at a time was small and hence it can be concluded the urge to travel was not driven solely for the trade. The Mojaves were tall and warlike. Many early accounts establish that the men averaged over six feet tall. The women tended to be much shorter and heavy set.

After a brief period of hostilities, the Mojaves were subdued in the spring of 1859 and Fort Mojave was established in their midst to guarantee their continued peacefulness. Fort Mojave was on the bluff across

23.

MILE 0.0 ON THE MOJAVE ROAD RECREATION TRAIL
A caravan lined up at Mile 0.0 at the Colorado River
ready for a tour over the Mojave Road. November 7,
1981.

Dennis Casebier Photo

24.

the river in Arizona. You are now standing in Nevada; and in fact, the first 11.2 miles of the Mojave Road are in Nevada. But the California and Nevada state line is only about two miles south of here.

Except for a brief interruption during the Civil War, when troops were needed elsewhere, Fort Mojave was maintained over on that bluff in Arizona until 1890, at which time the physical plant was turned over to the Interior Department and Fort Mojave became an Indian school. It remained an Indian school until the early 1930s. The buildings were demolished in 1941-1942.

Fort Mojave was the largest and most important army installation in this part of the California, Nevada, and Arizona desert country throughout the 1860s and 1870s. At times in the '60s, when the Hualpai War was in progress, as many as 500 men and hundreds of horses and mules to support them were stationed at Fort Mojave.

This site was an important crossing point of the Colorado River. Many of the early explorers, including Jedediah Strong Smith in 1826 and 1827 and Edward Fitzgerald Beale with his camels in 1857, crossed the river here. Once the fort was established, there was a ferry which lasted throughout the period that the wagon road and fort were active, and even on into the Indian school period. Another ferry was located up the river nine miles at Hardyville. The Hardyville ferry carried more traffic and was more elaborate than the Fort Mojave ferry. The one here was primitive, usually a scow guided by ropes but propelled across the river by Indians with poles and oars.

You are now ready to begin your drive over the Mojave Road. Head back west toward Pew Road over the road you took down here. (0.4 miles to next entry).

4   Pass through a little hollow with heavy brush. (0.6).

0   The first two miles west of the river pass through the flat floodplain adjacent to the Colorado River. Mud patches can form in the bottoms after heavy rains. Rains come here during the winter months from California Pacific storms, and during August and September, when Arizona receives heavy thunderstorms from the direction of the Gulf of California.

In prehistoric times the Colorado overflowed into this plain nearly every June or early July when the river would be as much as a mile wide. There were Mojave Indian rancherias in the floodplain. As the flood

25.

1.0   waters rose the Indians would pack up their few pos-
sessions and retreat, accompanied by rattlesnakes and
other denizens of the desert, to higher ground. As the
waters receded, the Indians would follow the edge of
the water planting in the lands that had been flooded in
somewhat the same way the ancient Egyptians planted in
the overflow of the Nile. Except for the spots cleared
by the Indians, this bottom was a tangle of trees and
vines. There was a lake here called Beaver Lake. It
was an ancient arm of the river. We pass a remnant of
the old lake. It is on the north (or right) side of the
road.

There is very little vegetation in the bottom land
now. This is because it is no longer watered, the
Colorado river being confined to a narrow channel.
There are skeletons of dead trees left from the days
when the river did overflow.

The water table is high enough that mesquite is
still growing in the bottoms. Both types native to the
Mojave Desert, screw bean and honey mesquite, are
found here. The mesquite beans were a major element in
the Mojaves' diet. They sustained themselves from their
own agriculture and from nature's contribution of
mesquite beans. There are also tamarisk trees and
arrow weed growing along with the mesquite. (0.7).

1.7   Leave the flat floodplain and begin to climb upward in a
wash directly west. There is a growth of smoke trees in
the wash. (1.3).

3.0   At about 3.0 miles from the river you come to the
blacktopped road that goes south to Needles (15.85
miles) or north to Nevada Highway 163 (10.6 miles).
Supplies and services of all kinds are available in
Needles. The road to the north provides access to
Laughlin, Nevada, Davis Dam, and Bullhead City,
Arizona. There are cairns on both sides of the highway
at this intersection, although during the first year of
their existence they were badly damaged twice. Please
repair them if they are down. There is loose sand
immediately to the west. Four-wheel drive is commonly
needed here, depending upon how your particular
vehicle is configured, on your driving skill, and on
how dry the sand is.

The von Schmidt historical marker is located just
off the highway at a point a little more than 3.3 miles
south toward Needles. You may have passed it on the
way from Needles, or you might want to take a quick
side trip down there to see this interesting monument.
The following account of the history of the von Schmidt

0   marker was provided by San Bernardino, California historian, Arda M. Haenszel.

"On the east side of River Road stands an iron post six feet high marking the first complete state boundary line. It is flanked by state historical plaques erected by both Nevada and California."

"There had been several earlier attempts to lay out the southeastern boundary of California, but it was Allexey Waldemar von Schmidt, in 1872, who ran the first legally recognized survey between Lake Tahoe and the Colorado River. This terminus was to be the point determined in 1861 by Lt. Joseph Christmas Ives, where the 35th parallel of north latitude crossed the mid-channel of the Colorado River. As might be expected, however, von Schmidt found that the current of the river had meanwhile altered its course in the floodplain, and he had to make adjustments."

"The monument shipped down the coast from San Francisco and up the Colorado by boat, was erected on the edge of the river terrace by the von Schmidt party. There is evidence that it was undercut by the wandering current in 1878 and toppled. It was apparently reestablished at a point as close as possible to the original one."

"The inscriptions cast in the four-sided von Schmidt monument are interesting. There are, of course, von Schmidt's name and the name of the San Francisco foundry where it was cast. The date is 1873, though the survey was actually completed a little ahead of expectations, in November 1872. The distance, 612 miles, refers to the length of the line from Lake Tahoe to the Colorado River. The north and south sides indicate Nevada and California, but on the west side "Oregon" is inscribed, referring to Oregon Territory. Since von Schmidt's day, the line has been resurveyed under more favorable conditions and with more accurate modern instruments. The present state line is about 3/4 mile farther north. However, the von Schmidt line was still considered significant enough to be marked, along with the present line, on the 1956 Homer Mountain 15' U.S.G.S. quadrangle map." (0.0+).

0+   Several roads were used to get up out of the Colorado River Valley in the old days. We've picked the one that is easiest to follow and which is most interesting and picturesque and the best preserved. There are quite a large number of smoke trees in the wash being followed here, though it is quite far north for them. They are more commonly thought of as a Colorado Desert plant.

27.

3.0+   At Mile 3.0 and beyond, creosote bushes dominate interspersed with rabbit brush. (0.4).

3.4   Pass under a north-south pole line, wooden poles, three wires. (0.4).

3.8   Road improves. Good road comes in from left. (0.9).

4.7   Cross under pole line again. Just after crossing under the wires, turn right in the general direction of the pole line. There will be cairns on the right. If you continue up the wash instead of turning right, it will take you up to the mouth of Picture Canyon, so named for the presence of prehistoric Indian petroglyphs. The Mojave Trail went this way before wagons were used. It is clear from Jedediah Strong Smith's journal that he went through Picture Canyon, although the presence of an expanding thicket of tamarisk is drawing the water table down. If you're not in a hurry, this is an interesting side trip. You can drive another 1.6 miles farther up the wash from this point (that is, 1.6 miles above Mile 4.7), after which the presence of bedrock makes hiking necessary (this 1.6 miles is very sandy). Bighorn sheep are sometimes seen watering in Picture Canyon. (0.4).

5.1   The remains of a small rock quarry are on the right of the road. The quarry may have been used by engineers as a rock source when dikes were being constructed along the Colorado River to control flooding. (0.1).

5.2   Since turning right at Mile 4.7 you have been following a well-marked road in a side wash. At Mile 5.2 the road to follow turns slightly to the right out of that wash. The wash continues to the left. We'll be rejoining that wash later. It cannot be followed by vehicle because it comes to a large, usually dry waterfall that cannot be ascended. In the old days, the wagons went the way we're going, while travelers on horseback and pack animals could continue up the wash. Angle to the right out of the wash. The road you're taking will lead you around the small conical hill you see on your left, and bring you back into the wash later. The washes in this area have not only smoke trees but also spiny catclaw. Also in evidence is the low dome-shaped shrub, brittle bush, with gray-green leaves and (at times) showy yellow-orange sunflowers extending well above the dome. (0.6).

5.8   The road is cut into soft uneven (but smooth) granite bedrock which produces a roller-coaster effect. Long wheelbase vehicles should proceed with caution. Nevertheless it's a good road. We're still basically proceeding in the same direction as the pole line, which parallels

CAMELS ON THE MOJAVE ROAD

No phase of Mojave Road history has captured the public fancy as much as the famous camel experiment of the late 1850s. From 1857-1860, camels were a familiar sight along the trail. The experiment "failed" (actually the camels did very well in our deserts) because the horses and mules were hysterically frightened of them and American teamsters didn't have the patience for the transition. Another factor was that the "father" of the camel experiment was U. S. Secretary of War Jefferson Davis. About the time a decision was needed regarding expanded use of camels in the American West, Davis became President of the Confederacy; hence, from a political standpoint, camels must be a bad idea. This photo and the one on the following page were taken on February 13, 1982, during a reenactment celebration on the Mojave Road.

Paul Lord Photo

FRIENDS OF THE MOJAVE ROAD AS CAMEL DRIVERS
Ed Manes and Bob Martin try their hands as camel drivers during the reenactment trek on the Mojave Road on February 13, 1982.

Paul Lord Photo

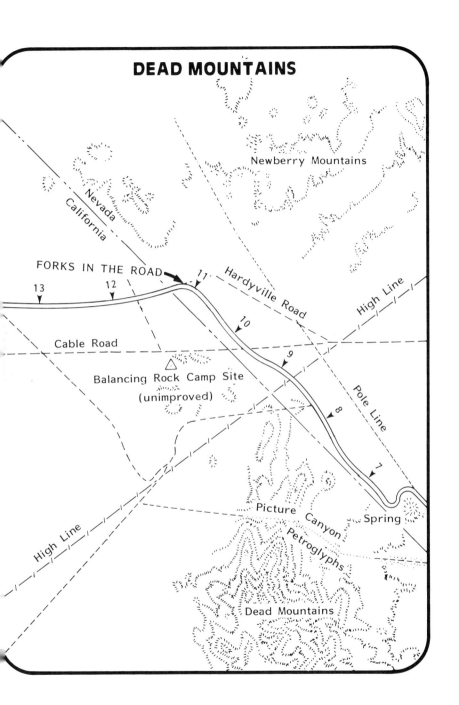

DEAD MOUNTAINS

Newberry Mountains

Nevada
California

FORKS IN THE ROAD

13

12

11

Hardyville Road

High Line

Cable Road

10

9

Balancing Rock Camp Site
(unimproved)

Pole Line

8

7

Picture Canyon

Spring

Petroglyphs

High Line

Dead Mountains

31.

5.8	us to the left. (0.3).
6.1	At this point, cross under pole line, then take a hard left, continuing the passage to the east and north of the conical hill on the left. You'll be leaving the pole line, which continues on north. Both roads are well traveled and hence there is the possibility of missing the turn. There are cairns at the intersection. (0.4).
6.5	Take a hard right as the road drops back into the wash you left at Mile 5.2. Generally, the road is well-traveled and hence easy to follow. If there has been a recent flood, it could be washed out. Floods of that magnitude are uncommon, but it can happen. To the left down the wash from this point approximately 200 yards is the dry waterfall referred to previously. Frequently, depending upon recent rainfall conditions, water seeps out through cracks in the rock. There are petroglyphs on rocks in this small canyon where the spring (called Granite Spring) occurs. As with the seep in Picture Canyon, increasing thickets of tamarisk are diminishing available surface water. Other signs of prehistoric occupation and use of the site will be seen if you hunt around. Now continue up this large wash that was just rejoined. (0.7).
7.2	Small cave near the bottom of the wash on the left (west side). Throughout this stretch you are in a large wash. Vegetation includes catclaw, creosote bush, smoke trees, paper bag bush (which has numerous swollen, papery dried fruits) and occasional ephedra. In the granite areas several types of barrel cactus and cholla can be seen. (0.6).
7.8	Yucca plants (Mohave Yucca) begin appearing. The appearance of this plant, of course, is a reflection of the gain we've made in altitude from about 550 feet at the Colorado River to about 1,800 feet at this point. (0.5).
8.3	The route of the wagon road you've been following turns to the right up out of the wash. A good road continues on up the wash to the left so this would be an easy point to go astray. Immediately after leaving the main wash, the wagon road bears northward hugging the eastern base of the ridge toward a highline. This is a tricky spot. We put quite a few cairns through here, so go slowly and make sure you're on the right track. (0.5).
8.8	Road passes under the highline. This is a major long-range power transmission line. The other lines we've passed under were lines using wooden poles. This one makes use of large-scale aluminum structures.

OFF-ROAD RACE ON THE MOJAVE ROAD
The "Laughlin 250" off-road race made use of segments of the Mojave Road in Nevada for several years. This use was considered to be inappropriate for the Mojave Road and, consequently, the race course has now been rerouted. This picture was taken near Mile 9.5 on February 25, 1984.
Dennis Casebier Photo

MOJAVE ROAD NEAR DEAD MOUNTAINS
A stretch of the Mojave Road (looking southeast) at about Mile 8. Photo was taken the day after the Laughlin 250 Off-Road Race. The road was restored to original condition a few days later. Two cairns, erected by volunteers, are visible on the left. This photo is backwards for people traveling from east to west.
Dennis Casebier Photo

A small prospect hole is just above the level of the wash on the right. The density of yucca plants increases. The road enters an area where creosote bush and burrobush grow in association. The burrobush is a low, dense, gray foliaged shrub with intricately branched, white-barked stems. (0.3).

A pretty "teddy bear" cholla patch is to the right of the road. (0.3).

Route of the old road crosses the Underground Telephone Cable Road. That road is maintained almost like an improved county road. If you turn right, it'll take you back to the Needles Highway in 6.0 miles (east). To the left it'll take you to U. S. Highway 95 in 4.2 miles. About 1.0 miles to the left is the primitive camp site called Balancing Rock Camp Site. When you hit this intersection, the old road approaches at a shallow angle, so it is easy to get side-tracked off on the Cable Road. Remember, the old Mojave Road goes directly across. There are cairns to show the way. The Mojave Road doesn't travel any appreciable distance (only about 100 ft.) on the Cable Road.

The underground telephone cable was put in during the early 1960s. It is a product of the first round of world-wide nuclear war scares. The cable was buried sufficiently deep so it could be expected to survive a nuclear attack. The plan was that, as we all die slow deaths from various forms of blast effects and radiation exposure, we'll be able to talk with one another from coast-to-coast over this cable. It is still active and regularly patrolled by low-flying aircraft. If you happen to be close to the Cable Road and find yourself being buzzed by a plane, that's probably what it's all about.

This is about the last possibility to go astray between here and U. S. Highway 95, which is 4.6 miles ahead on the old road. Beyond the Cable Road the Mojave Road is a little more sandy than it has been to this point. Creosote bushes, yuccas, and a few chollas are in evidence.

Along this stretch we have a good view of the Newberry Mountains (or Spirit Mountain) to the north and the Dead Mountains to the south. Both of these ranges are sacred to the Mojave Indians. The north-south line of these mountains marks the western boundary of their aboriginal territory. The country from here to Piute Creek was a sort of no-man's land, so far as Indians of the recent prehistoric period were concerned. The Piutes and Chemehuevis lived on the

35.

9.7 west and the Mojaves claimed the land to the east.

The Piutes and Chemehuevis were the Indians of the desert. In contrast to the Mojaves, who gained their subsistence largely from agriculture, the Piutes and Chemehuevis lived by hunting and gathering. They moved around the desert in response to ripening of seeds and nuts and the availability of game. They endured a "hand to mouth" existence, whereas the agricultural pursuits of the Mojaves provided them with a more certain subsistence. In prehistoric times, the Mojaves were by far the more powerful tribe. They would pass with impunity through the country of the desert Indians. When it came to warfare with the whites, it soon became apparent that the Piutes and Chemehuevis enjoyed a tactical advantage in the form of their more extensive real estate holdings.

The Mojaves controlled, or "owned," only the valley of the Colorado River; they had no extensive desert mountains to which they could flee. On the other hand, the Chemehuevis and Piutes could melt into the vastness of their desert wilderness and carry on a guerrilla warfare against the whites. Consequently, the Mojaves were by far the first to capitulate (they either had to stand and fight, or surrender), while the Chemehuevis held out for several years longer, making attacks on white travelers and scattered settlers.

It can be noted that as far as wagon roads are concerned, the stretch you have traveled over so far was considered to be quite easy. In fact, the entire 23 miles from the river to Piute Creek was good road. Most wagons that were used on this road, including stages, were drawn by mules or, somewhat less commonly but still not rare, horses. There were some oxen teams, but very few. In the early days, eight mules constituted the average team. Later 12, 16, and even larger numbers of mules were used as one team. (1.1).

10.8 For a short distance (50 feet or so) the road divides. This was done in 1984 during practice sessions of the Laughlin 250 Off-Road Vehicle Race. Segments of the Mojave Road were used for the race that year. There are few remaining signs. (0.3).

11.1 Forks of the Road. This was an important junction in the old days. The branch to the right is the Hardyville Road, and there was a way by which either Fort Mojave or Hardyville could be reached on this road. The Hardyville road is not presently planned for recreational use. There is a large cairn in the fork of the "Y" with an iron post in the center. Our road turns west (left)

1   here. (0.1).
2   California & Nevada State Line. It is not prominently
     marked. Nearing the crest of the pass between the
     Newberry Mountains and the Dead Mountains, the
     predominate plants are wild buckwheat, creosote bush,
     and desert sunflower, which is readily identified by its
     triangular, toothed leaves and flower heads that extend
     well above the leaves on long stems. (0.1).
3   This is the high point in the pass (the altitude is 2,680
     feet, more than 2,000 feet above where we started at
     the Colorado River). From this point you get your first
     glimpse of the Piute Range to the west. It is easy to
     tell where Fort Piute and Piute Creek are because,
     looking west, there is a slight break in the Piute
     Mountains at that point. Far beyond, generally showing
     a hazy blue even on clear days, Table Top Mountain is
     positioned directly in that notch. This point also pro-
     vides a good view of the north end of the Dead Moun-
     tains on your left (or south) and the Newberry Moun-
     tains on your right (or north). The view of the
     Newberrys is not as unobstructed as that of the Dead
     Mountains. Driving down to the west into Piute Valley
     toward U. S. Highway 95, the dominant shrubs are
     creosote bush, burrobush, desert sunflower, Mohave
     yucca, wild buckwheat, and silver cholla. (0.3).
6   The Underground Telephone Cable Road is plainly
     visible crossing Piute Valley, which now stretches out
     right and left in front of you. As you continue, there
     is a fine view of the Piute Range beyond, one of the
     truly magnificent scenic and natural wilderness areas of
     the East Mojave. To the southwest is Homer Mountain.
     Piute Valley runs north toward Searchlight, Nevada,
     and south to Needles, California.
          For the next mile or so there are major undulations
     in the road. The surface is hard, but these dips are
     sharp and some quite short. Consequently, a vehicle
     with a long wheelbase or long rear overhang should
     proceed with caution. There are 10 mph stretches along
     here. (0.1)
7   Faint north-south trail crossing. During World War II
     literally millions of American servicemen were trained in
     the California deserts for combat duty in battlefields
     around the world. Among the first were General George
     S. Patton and his command, destined for the deserts of
     North Africa. Many others would come after them. The
     region used by them was called the Desert Training
     Center and later the California-Arizona Maneuver Area.
     The northernmost extension of the DTC or C-AMA was

37.

MOTORCYCLISTS ON THE MOJAVE ROAD
This scene is near Mile 11.6 looking northeast toward
the south end of the Newberry Mountains.
Dennis Casebier Photo

MOJAVE ROAD IN PIUTE VALLEY
Looking west along the Mojave Road near Mile 12.7 across the broad expanse of Piute Valley. The Piute Mountains are on the horizon stretching across the picture. Piute Creek is in those mountains just a little left of center. November 27, 1981.
Dennis Casebier Photo

11.7   here in Piute Valley. The region passed through now
        must have been a minor impact area since shrapnel has
        been seen here. There could still be unexploded ord-
        nance and if you see any, don't approach it; instead,
        simply note its location and report the find to BLM.
        (0.6).
12.3   Road leaves the worst of the undulations referred to
        above. (1.4).
13.7   A private drive takes off to the right. It should be
        avoided unless you are invited by the residents. From
        this point to U. S. Highway 95, the condition of our
        road is much improved because it is maintained by the
        private landowners. Experimentation with jojoba farming
        is underway in this region to the north of our roadway.
        (0.6).
14.3   U. S. Highway 95. To the right (north) the distance to
        Searchlight, Nevada is 24.8 miles. To the left (south)
        the distance to Arrowhead Junction and the Santa Fe
        Railroad is 11.8 miles (no services at that point). The
        total distance to Needles via Arrowhead Junction is 28.5
        miles (that is, 11.8 miles to Arrowhead Junction, 5.6
        miles from Arrowhead Junction to I-40, and then 11.1
        miles on I-40 to Needles). (0.+).
14.3+   It is always a thrill to see wildlife on the desert.
        You're almost sure to encounter an assortment of liz-
        ards, rabbits, hawks, and snakes during your journey
        on the trail. If you're fortunate, and depending largely
        on the time of year, you'll see a great variety of wild-
        life. The valley ahead of you is a particularly good
        place to see desert tortoises when the season and time
        of day are right. Once, for example, when we passed
        through here early in the morning in April, we saw 18
        desert tortoises on the road between Miles 14 and 20!
        We have seen fairly large numbers of them in this
        region at other times. Of course, they should not be
        disturbed at all. We don't hesitate to photograph them,
        even at close range, but they shouldn't be picked up
        since they may become upset and discharge their stored
        water supply. The tortoise is the California State
        reptile. It is protected by law. Many consider these
        animals to be endangered. They deserve our considera-
        tion and protection; certainly they lend a distinctive
        charm to the desert environment and are always fun to
        see. Research suggests, however, that there may be
        more desert tortoises now than there were in prehistoric
        times. This is because they were relentlessly pursued
        by the Chemehuevis Indians being highly coveted as a
        delicacy. The Indians would take a live tortoise, lay

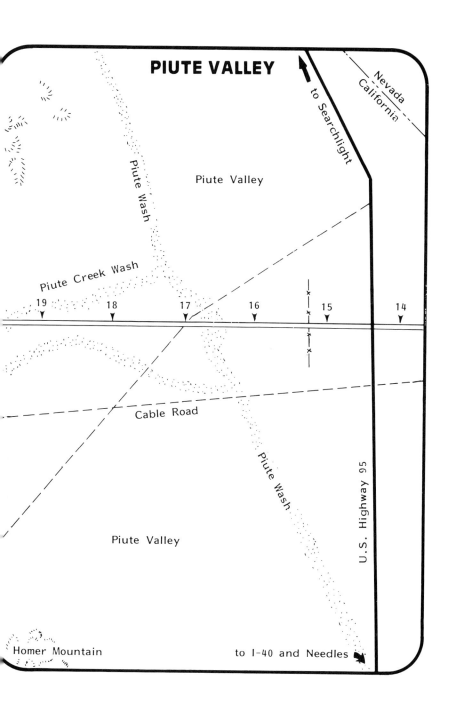

PIUTE VALLEY

Nevada
California

to Searchlight

Piute Valley

Piute Wash

Piute Creek Wash

19 18 17 16 15 14

Cable Road

Piute Wash

U.S. Highway 95

Piute Valley

Homer Mountain

to I-40 and Needles

41.

14.3+   him on his back on hot coals, and prepare tortoise stew right in the shell! Please admire, photograph, and love these wonderful animals, but do not disturb them. Do not remove them from the desert. And don't consider developing a taste for tortoise stew! (0.9).

15.2   The road passes through a range fence. There are tall posts on both sides of the cattle guard. This is one of the many fence lines you'll see in the East Mojave. They are used by cattlemen to divide the range. Cattle are moved around in response to the availability of grass. On November 12, 1985, a cattle guard was erected here by volunteers from the California Association of Four Wheel Drive Clubs; as a result of their efforts, it will not be necessary for you to open and close a gate. (1.3).

16.5   Road approaches the east side of Piute Wash. Impressive flash floods can rush down this wash. Caution should be exercised in crossing the wash whenever rain might be falling in any part of the widespread watershed. Of course, camping in washes is always discouraged because of the possibility of unexpected flash floods, especially at night. Most washes in the East Mojave are "Great Basin" washes; that is, they empty, eventually, into lakes that have no outlet to the sea. Piute Wash is one of the few exceptions. Draining the immense Piute Valley, it flows south for many miles, then turns east around the south end of the Dead Mountains. It joins the Colorado River just above Needles, and then flows with that river to the Gulf of California and the Pacific Ocean. (0.3).

16.8   Road leaves west edge of Piute Wash. (0.2).

17.0   Faint road crosses NE-SW. Continue due west as indicated by cairns. Enter a stretch of the road that has had blade work done on it. This is believed to date from World War II Desert Training Center days. We didn't put many cairns across Piute Valley because we felt they were not needed. (2.2).

19.2   Road crosses fairly large washes. Blow sand collects in them. It should be noted that these washes drain Piute Creek. Heavy rains in Lanfair Valley or on the Piute Range can cause extremely heavy flash floods in these washes. (1.3).

20.5   Cross a north-south road. Continue west. From this point to the north-south Metropolitan Water District High Line, which is visible at a distance of about one mile, the road is rougher and more difficult to follow. It will continue to be rough and rocky all the way to Piute Creek and Fort Piute. Proceed slowly and watch

42.

.5   closely for cairns. Looking straight ahead, you'll notice a small conical hill detached from the main line of the mountains (Jedediah Smith Butte -- or sometimes called Lookout Mountain). In the old days the wagon road went to the left (south) of the butte. That route is not passable now because of changes brought about by flash floods in Piute Creek. We'll be traveling in a slightly more northerly direction and will pass to the north of Jed Smith Butte because of the amount of labor involved and for preservation considerations. It would result in considerable damage to the environment with no real gain to us. (0.4).

.9   You'll come to three cairns. This is the point at which you'll have to bend slightly to the right. You'll see a trace of a road angling to the left at this point. That is the old road that we have abandoned for reasons stated. Take the route that bends to the right. (0.6).

.5   Road reaches the Metropolitan Water District Power Line, a major complex with metal structures. CAUTION: Vehicles must dead-end at Mile 23.5, 0.1 miles beyond Fort Piute ruins, and return to this point. Hikers may continue, however, and be picked up on the other side of the mountains. (0.+).

.5+   Continuing west from the power line, there are several paths that can be taken on to Piute Creek. All are rough and rocky, so drive very slowly from the power line to Piute Creek. These roads all come together at about Mile 22.2, a point north of Jed Smith Butte. (1.1).

.6   A road comes in from the left (south) that angles across Piute Creek and back over to the MWD power line in a southeasterly direction. This road is extremely rough and at times impassable because of washouts where it crosses Piute Creek. Sometimes there is a locked gate along it. There is no reason to take it. It should be avoided. Continue west toward Piute Creek and Fort Piute. (0.3).

.9   A driveway leads to the left. Generally this is blocked by a post and cable barricade put up several years ago to prevent vehicles from driving down below, where there are petroglyphs. The ruins you see down to the left a few hundred feet are what is left of the George Irwin Ranch. Nearly 140 acres of land around Piute Creek are not in the public domain. These key acres presently belong to the California Department of Fish and Game. The site was originally homesteaded in the late 1920s and finally patented by Thomas W. Van Slyke in 1930. Van Slyke had a brother who sometimes lived

43.

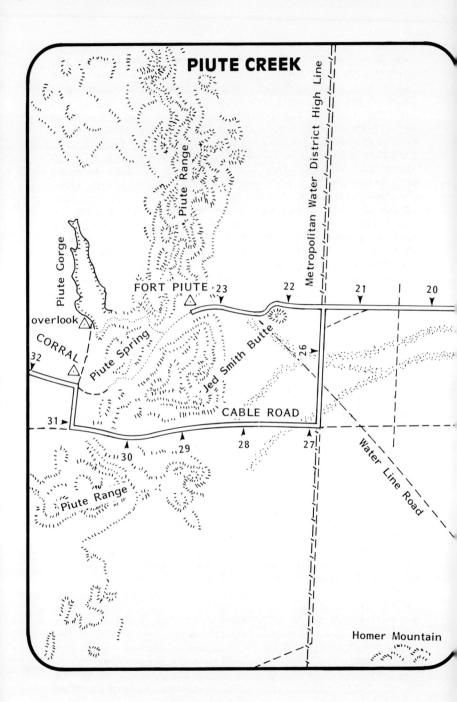

PIUTE CREEK

Piute Range

Metropolitan Water District High Line

Piute Gorge

overlook

FORT PIUTE ◢ 23

22 ▾

21 ▾

20 ▾

CORRAL

32 ▾

Piute Spring

Jed Smith Butte

26 ▾

31 ▾

CABLE ROAD

30 ▾

29 ▾

28 ▾

27 ▾

Piute Range

Water Line Road

Homer Mountain

44.

.9 with him. They built a house out of 1X12s that was dug into the north bank of Piute Creek (just below the point where you turn down to Irwin Ranch ruins). The house was burned in the 1950s by parties unknown and for reasons that only they understood. Van Slyke and his brother were prospectors and miners. In 1944, when Van Slyke was about 73 years of age, he sold the 140 acres to which he had gained patent to George and Virginia Irwin. The Irwins built a home using local stone and railroad ties and set about to raise turkeys and experiment with agricultural products. They built the turkey pens that have survived to the present time as ruins. The remains of their home are still visible on the bench below where you're driving now, near the turkey pens. The Irwins battled with bobcats and coyotes to determine whether they or the predators of the desert would reap the harvest. In about two years, it was conceded that the denizens had won. George Irwin went to work as a lineman on the Metropolitan Water District highline between Hoover Dam and the Iron Mountain pumping station. He then moved his family to Camino, which is near Needles. (0.1).

.0 There is a "Y" in the road. Take either branch. They rejoin in a few hundred yards. Both are rough. (0.4).

4 The stone ruin up to the right is the remains of what is commonly called "Fort Piute." You will be able to drive only a few hundred feet more. (0.1).

5 Just across the wash (up canyon) from Fort Piute, there are the ruins of a stone corral. This is old, too, but probably doesn't date back to the 1860s when Fort Piute was built.

DO NOT UNDER ANY CIRCUMSTANCES ATTEMPT TO DRIVE BEYOND MILE 23.5

Do not attempt to drive upstream beyond the ruins of the rock corral. The road is impassable. In the old days, the wagon road went up the stream bed. This route is blocked now by trees and waterfalls. There is no way to get a vehicle through. If you make the attempt, you will do damage to your vehicle, the environment, and possibly to yourself.

To continue on west along the Mojave Road with a vehicle, it is necessary to backtrack 2.0 miles to the MWD power line road, then 1.4 miles south on it to the Cable Road, then 4.0 miles westward through the Piute Mountains to a cattle guard and fence line, then to the right (north) 0.5 miles, where cairns will show that

45.

PREHISTORIC INDIAN PETROGLYPHS
The Piute Creek area is a museum of prehistoric Indian art. You must spend many days there to locate and see it all and to begin to understand this wonderful site. May 21, 1973.

Dennis Casebier Photo

46.

PREHISTORIC INDIAN PETROGLYPHS
These are at Piute Creek. They are found in many
places and with many forms along the Mojave Road.

47.

23.5   you're back on the Mojave Road.

     Many visitors will spend extra time in the Piute Creek region. There is much to see. Also, it may be convenient to let part of your party hike over Piute Hill while those who remain take the vehicles around. They can get back together at the base of Piute Hill on the west side. It is a fascinating hike, but quite strenuous. Allow at least two hours for the hike over the hill, depending upon the condition of the hikers and the amount of time you've got to spend. A special Piute Creek Recreational Area Map is provided on the following pages.

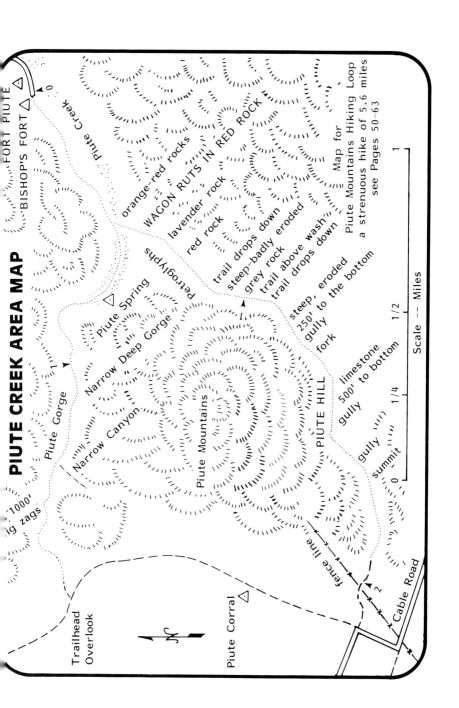

PIUTE CREEK AREA MAP

FORT PIUTE
BISHOP'S FORT

Piute Creek
Piute Creek

orange-red rocks
WAGON RUTS IN RED ROCK
lavender rock
red rock

Piute Spring

petroglyphs

Narrow Deep Gorge

Piute Gorge

Narrow Canyon

Piute Mountains

trail drops down
steep-badly eroded
grey rock
trail above wash
trail drops down

steep, eroded
250' to the bottom
gully
fork

Map for
Piute Mountains Hiking Loop
a strenuous hike of 5.6 miles
see Pages 50-63

PIUTE HILL

limestone
500' to bottom
gully

gully

summit

Scale -- Miles

1/4   1/2   1

fence line

Cable Road

'1000'
ig zags

Trailhead
Overlook

Piute Corral

49.

PIUTE MOUNTAINS HIKING LOOP

There is a wonderful hiking loop that can be taken at Fort Piute if you've got the time and energy. The measurements for this were made in the field by Chuz and Dick Howard, Pat and Terry Davison, and Mike and Kenneth Commissaris. Chuz, Terry, and Mike then assisted Pat in writing up the following hiking guide.

Background Information

1. Approximate distances: Fort Piute to Piute Creek bottom 0.6 miles. Piute Creek through Piute Gorge to base of Piute Hill 2.5 miles. Piute Hill back to Fort Piute 2.5 miles. Total distance for the entire hike 5.6 miles.
2. The Homer Mountain and Lanfair Valley 15" U.S.G.S. topographic maps cover the area of the hike.
3. Plan most of a day for the hike. It is a moderate hike, but takes at least six hours.
4. Be prepared. Wear boots and sufficient clothing to protect yourself from the elements of nature (snakes included!). Insect repellant is advised for the hike along Piute Creek. Take at least one quart of water per person (more if it is a warm day).
5. The map and narrative will guide you. Read the narrative and study the map before starting. The stated distances are approximations -- use the references to landmarks too.
6. Even though it may look possible, don't consider driving east down from the summit of Piute Hill. This hiking trail allows us to enjoy an unaltered, untraveled, original section of the Mojave Road. The trail is a means of preserving the wagon road.
7. No matter how tempting it might appear, the water in Piute Creek is not considered fit to drink.

FORT PIUTE

We call this area "Fort Piute," but actually the structures and documents show that Piute was never called "fort" by the U. S. Army. To them it was the "Outpost at Piute Creek." It was built in 1867-1868.

FORT PIUTE TO PIUTE CREEK

Find a parking spot near the ruins of the fort or by the corral. The trail begins at the historical

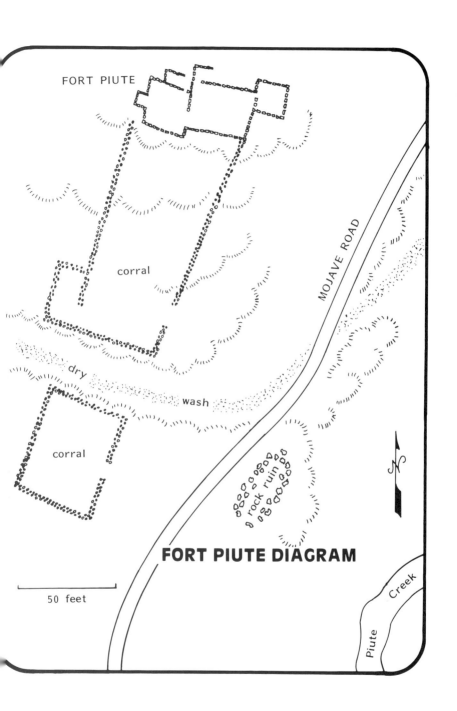

FORT PIUTE

corral

dry

wash

MOJAVE ROAD

corral

rock ruin

FORT PIUTE DIAGRAM

50 feet

Creek

Piute

51.

FORT PIUTE

A view taken inside the ruins of Fort Piute looking east
across Piute Valley. Conical-shaped Jedediah Smith
Butte -- sometimes called Lookout Mountain -- guards
the entrance to the Piute Creek area. May 7, 1974.

Dennis Casebier Photo

PIUTE PASS
The army maintained an outpost at Piute Creek in 1867 and 1868 to protect the Arizona Overland Mail from roving bands of desert Indians. This view was taken in 1973 inside the ruins of the main fort building looking southwest toward Piute Pass. The notorious Piute Hill is just left of the small dark peaks on the horizon.

Dennis Casebier Photo

CHEMEHUEVIS HUT AT PIUTE CREEK
The "Chemehuevi Hut" at Piute Creek. The photo was
taken on one of Malcom J. Rogers' visits to the area,
probably in 1929.
San Diego Museum of Man Collections

54.

ns. (Pàh-Utahs.)

CHEMEHUEVI INDIAN
A Drawing from the 1850s

55.

monument east of the fort. Elevation at the fort is 2,800 feet. Follow the vehicle road up the canyon, passing the old corral in ruins on the right. It is uncertain whether these ruins date from 1867 when the outpost was built, but in any case they are quite old. The vehicle road ends at the gully about 260' from the corral. Do not attempt to drive beyond this point under any circumstances! Stay out of the stream bed and follow the trail straight ahead. Indian petroglyphs can be seen approximately 250' from the end of the road on the right side of the hill as well as farther on in the middle of the trail.

At a distance of 300' from the petroglyphs, a wall of large rocks is the next landmark. This wall is believed to be the remains of Samuel Bishop's fort. Samuel Bishop was camped with his men in the Piute area in 1859 and may have erected the stone structure. Bishop's party was assisting Edward F. Beale who was under contract with the War Department to survey and establish a wagon road route along the 35th Parallel of North Latitude. On April 5th and 6th, 1859, Bishop's men cached some supplies here which they intended to retrieve later. Several companies of soldiers came through at the end of April shortly after Bishop and his men had left. The hungry soldiers came upon Bishop's caches and the supplies didn't last long, but the dispute between Bishop and the Army did last and, in fact, it was never truly resolved.

Another noteworthy item at this site was the discovery in 1973 of a large stone with the name "S. A. Bishop" inscribed upon it. The stone has since been tumbled into Piute Creek and broken. To prevent loss of such a valuable relic, the stone was removed by the Bureau of Land Management, later reconstructed, and is now on display at the Mojave River Valley Museum in Barstow.

Spanning the stream bed at this point are the remains of an old concrete dam. The dam has a somewhat more recent history. The dam formed what was known as "the best swimming hole for miles around."

Back at Bishop's fort, a fork divides the trail. Take the right fork -- the left fork is probably one of the old wagon roads down to the creek. Soon the trail meanders above the creek along the edge of a cliff, and in fact it continues above Piute Creek for about 0.4 miles. Another fork presents itself 800' from Bishop's fort. Take the right fork and continue along, about 380' or so. Then you come to another fork -- again go

PIUTE CREEK
Each day a quarter-of-a-million gallons of good potable
water magically rises from the sand and begins a
mile-long run through an isolated desert canyon creat-
ing an oasis that is a delight to all the denizens of the
desert. April 14, 1973.
Dennis Casebier Photo

right. On the trail approximately 110' from the last mentioned fork is a large rock with the letters IHPL inscribed above the letters SAO. Follow the trail 150' past the lettered rock and you come upon a black rock outcropping. Then go 400' farther and notice another trail, seemingly well worn, coming in from the right. Remember, you are still up above the creek.

Only 150' past the trail junction is a fork going down (left) to the creek bottom. The trail straight ahead stays above the creek, but you want to drop down, so take the left fork. This first part of the trail ends down in the creek bed about 110' from the start of the descent. Cairns should be found along this descent and in the stream bed. At this point the trail through Piute Gorge takes off to the right; the trail over Piute Hill intersects the creek bottom 150' to the left.

Piute Creek -- Piute Gorge
Lanfair Valley -- Piute Hill

At the creek bottom, turn right (northwest) up the canyon. The trail will stay in this canyon until you reach the turn to climb up into Lanfair Valley on the opposite (west) side of the Piute Mountains. Follow the wash through sometimes dense and almost impenetrable growths of willows, tules, and assorted plant life. Insects can be quite bothersome here, so be prepared. Several side trails come in along the path, but stay in the creek bed. Approximately 1/3rd of a mile from the starting point, the trail passes Piute Spring, most recognizable by the abundance of willows, rushes, and cottonwood trees. Beyond that the wash then becomes dry. Follow the wash up through the gorge and enjoy the beautiful scenery. Golden eagles are sometimes seen in this canyon. Big horn sheep sometimes come down to Piute Creek to water.

It is easy to imagine yourself back in the 1860s traveling on horseback and feeling anxious to reach Lanfair Valley. You would have to be careful and watchful. The gorge is a perfect spot for an ambush! The high walls offer no protection to the traveler below except from the sun in early morning and late afternoon. Because the walls are so close together at points in the canyon, travelers with wagons would have to use the Piute Hill route to reach Lanfair Valley instead of the narrow gorgeway you are now hiking.

The trail climbs over rock ledges and dry

PIUTE GORGE

The canyon in which Piute Creek occurs is cut directly through the mountains and originates as a depression in Lanfair Valley on the west side. Travelers without wagons went this way rather than tackle Piute Hill. Remnants of the old trail can be seen at the point where it climbed out of the depression. July 11, 1974.

Dennis Casebier Photo

PIUTE HILL

Piute Hill, one of the worst hills on the wagon roads of the West. By traveling a short distance to the south, the worst of the mountains could have been crossed with less difficulty, but the distance to water would have been increased, and that was the driving force in determining the route of early desert highways. July 1974.

Dennis Casebier Photo

waterfalls between stretches of sand. Hard to miss is the sharp red rock jutting out, and farther on, a red streak in the rock is running diagonally up the right side of the canyon wall. Approximately 1,200' from the red streaked wall, the trail winds around a huge trapezoidal rock. Then, 900' past that rock, the wash meets up with a deep canyon on the left. It looks like an old eroded horse trail. Stay in the main dry wash, passing a cairn on the right 50' from the outlet of the side canyon. The trail weaves back and forth for 1,000'. A cairn marks the spot where the hiker should turn left, leaving the wash and following an old pack trail up the side of the gorge. Approximately 1,100' from the bottom, the trail reaches the flat plain of Lanfair Valley with a view back towards Piute Gorge. About 150' from the trailhead, you come across a road. Take the road left (south) 0.9 miles to the crossroads at the base of Piute Hill (this is Mile 31.4) on the Mojave Road Recreation Trail). On the way you pass an old corral (called Piute Corral by the cattle company that owns it) and usually you will have this entire area to yourself. The crossroads might be a good spot to eat lunch, but you won't find any shade! Elevation at the crossroads is 3,440 feet.

Piute Hill -- Piute Creek -- Fort Piute

Standing at the crossroads marked with cairns, you turn left and look up (northeast) to the relatively easy west side of Piute Hill. It is the east side of this hill that was so feared by early travelers who called it "precipitous," "impractical," and "dangerous." Walking on the trail toward Piute Hill, you make several turns and come to a cattle gate about 1,300' from the crossroads. The wagon road may not have had the turns encountered here, but these are necessary to make use of the gateway in the range fence. Make sure you close the gate. About 160' past the cattle gate is a road branching off to the right. It deadends 0.7 miles from the branch. There are loose rocks and natural obstacles in the pathway, so hike cautiously. Stay on the main trail and continue the climb. It is about 1,700' from the cattle gate to the top of Piute Hill. There is a slight bend and then you have reached the top of the pass, elevation 3,570', crowned with rock cairns. The road continues down the other side to the left. It is all downhill now, crossing gullies and curving along the hillside.

61.

PIUTE CREEK AREA
This 1974 view of the Piute Creek area was taken from the heights above the canyon to the west.
Dennis Casebier Photo

There apparently were at least three routes the wagons used at different times on the east side of Piute Hill. The trail follows the most visible and the one that had the most terracing work on the steep hillside. Traces of the other two are noticeable to the right (south), past the summit.

This section of the Mojave Road was particularly hazardous (uphill and downhill) because of the terrain, and when Indians were involved, the hazards were greatly increased.

About one-half mile from the summit, the trail passes a section of limestone outcroppings. Soon after (in 450'), the trail forks at a gully crossing. This gully is the third from the summit and the last to be crossed on the descent to Piute Creek. The fork to the right goes down the gully to the wash below. Stay on the main road. You are drawing closer to the wash, and 700' from the gully fork, the trail drops down into the gravelly wash. Stay in the wash for the next 470', at which point the trail rises slightly above the wash. The surrounding rock is grey. Continue above the wash about 450'; then the trail again drops down to the wash and the surrounding rock is red. Petroglyphs can be spotted on the left side. Cairns are placed along the wash, and the trail follows the wash for about 860'. The trail then turns left out of the wash and passes an area of lavender rock. Keep your eyes open. DO NOT CONTINUE TO FOLLOW THE WASH.

About 450' from the lavender rock is a part of the road that proves wagons used it. Very noticeable on the trail is a stretch of orange-red rock with two well-worn ruts from the wagon wheels. This spot is a good place to take pictures and these ruts bring into clear focus the hardships and rigors the early desert travelers had to overcome. Near the wagon wheel marks, petroglyphs can be found on both sides of the trail.

The cool (but not drinkable) water of Piute Creek is only about 150 feet ahead. Once down in the creek bottom, go 150 feet left (northwest) to the cairn marking the trail up the opposite side of the creek, taking you back to the ruins of the fort the way you came.

23.5   To continue on westward along the Mojave Road Recreation Trail from Piute Creek you must double back to the
east (back the way you came) for 2.0 miles to the
Metropolitan Water District Power Line Road. (2.0).

25.5   Intersection with the MWD Power Line Road. Head south
along the power line road. It is assumed that if you
planned to visit the Piute Creek area, you've already
done that, and now you're back on the MWD road as
indicated. (0.5).

26.0   Cross a wash. This is the streambed of Piute Creek.
All the water that comes down through Piute Canyon
flows through this wash. If you should happen to be
here when it is raining in Lanfair Valley or on the
Piute Mountains, you might not be able to pass. MWD
generally keeps this service road in good condition, but
floods coming down Piute Creek can wash the road out
at this point. 4WDs can generally get across anyway,
but it can be extremely rough. Piute Creek seldom runs
on the surface beyond this point except after heavy
rains, but at such times the stream may continue on the
surface here for several months. (0.3).

26.3   Cross another wash. This is the streambed for the wash
that drains the next canyon south in the Piute Range.
You'll be following it on the Cable Road to cross the
mountains. This wash, too, can carry heavy flash
floods and wash out the MWD road. (0.1).

26.4   Off to the right approximately 100 yards is a water
tank, and at this point a straight road running northwest and southeast passes. This is a water line road. It
was put in by the OX Cattle Company years ago to
convey water through plastic pipes (buried beneath the
road) from Piute Creek out into Piute Valley, thereby
extending the grazing range for cattle far out into the
valley where, in most years, there is sufficient forage
for that purpose. Continue straight ahead. (0.3).

26.7   Cross another wash that comes out of the Piute Mountains. (0.2).

26.9   Intersection with the Cable Road. Turn right or due
west on the Cable Road. Of course, this is the same
Underground Telephone Cable Road that we crossed
near the north end of the Dead Mountains at Mile 9.7.
We'll cross it several more times and it'll stay fairly
close to us most of the way across the East Mojave,
until we reach Seventeenmile Point at Mile 88.0, where
the two routes finally diverge. ((0.0+).

26.9+   As you head up Piute Mountains, the density of yucca

9+ increases considerably. Along with the Mohave Yucca there are buckhorn cholla, barrel cactus, and pencil cholla. The slope is quite rocky, and the road can be fairly bumpy. As with the MWD and their power line road, the Pacific Telephone Company keeps the Cable Road in good condition. However, if there have been floods since it was last serviced, there can be wash-outs. There are steep grades and dropoffs on this stretch over the Piute Range. If you're unfamiliar with the road, you should drive with special caution. (1.7).

6 On the right (north) you'll see a small metal building. This is a service structure for the Cable Road. They appear at intervals along the road. The buildings are marked "off limits." Most of them have numbers on their roofs, and therefore can serve as reference points or landmarks. The one at this point has K11 on the roof. (0.7).

3 Cross the main wash in this canyon. There is a small patch of asphalt on the road to provide protection from the effects of flooding. (0.0+).

3+ As you proceed up through this pass, there is a beau-tiful view of fairly old igneous rocks in different shades of red and brown off to the right (north). Of course, this entire mountain range is volcanic in origin. Also, as you ascend, the amount of vegetation increases significantly, achieving what is sometimes called "gar-den" proportions on the desert. There are thick stands of staghorn cholla (or deerhorn or buckhorn), barrel cactus, and yucca. In the spring, at the right time and in the right years, there can be heavy growths of wildflowers on these slopes. (1.2).

5 Summit. You cross over the Piute Range at this point and are treated to a wonderful view of Lanfair Valley. (0.4).

9 Range fence. There's a cattle guard across the road. Turn right (north) immediately beyond the cattle guard. (0.5).

4 Intersect the Mojave Road. You're out in a fairly large open area against the west side of the Piute Range that has very little vegetation. Apparently this is the an-cient bed of a small lake. Enough chemicals were con-centrated here by evaporating waters that very little vegetation grows now. The Mojave Road is quite faint here as it crosses right and left. At this point, you have a choice. You can turn left and continue your journey along the Mojave Road toward the west, or you can turn right and go to the crest of the trail coming up the mountain from Piute Creek. The mileage Guide

31.4   assumes you turn left and continue.

To visit the crest of Piute Hill turn right. The Mojave Road wanders a little to the left to reach a gate in the same range fence that we passed through at mile 30.9. There are tall poles on either side of the gate. If you get a little confused here, look up and down the fence line for the tall poles and remember you've got to go through them. Generally the gate between these poles is closed, and if so, you'll have to close it as you leave it. It is recommended that you not drive beyond this point. A fairly short hike (short, but steep) will take you to the top of the hill. There is little room for maneuvering vehicles at the top, and the danger of doing damage to the hill or to the vehicles in getting them up the hill is significant. It is completely impractical for larger groups of vehicles, say more than three, to drive up under any circumstances. And it is recommended that no one drive up.

Now go through the gate. The road is rough, steep, and rocky.

TOP OF PIUTE HILL OR PIUTE MOUNTAIN. To the east, the old Mojave Road plunges down Piute Mountain toward Piute Creek. YOU CANNOT DRIVE DOWN PIUTE HILL WITHOUT DOING DAMAGE TO YOUR VEHICLE AND THE ENVIRONMENT AND POSSIBLY TO YOURSELF! DO NOT ATTEMPT TO DRIVE DOWN PIUTE HILL. As already mentioned, it makes a wonderful hike. The hiking loop that can be taken is explained elsewhere in the Guide. It can be commenced here as well as from the fort or other points.

If you'll look off to the north, you'll see quite a gorge on the west side of the Piute Range at a distance of about a mile. That gorge is cut completely through the range. The hiking loop might start with your vehicle parked on the edge of the gorge. You could hike from there over to where you're standing now, by way of the Piute Corral you see out in the flat, and then hike down Piute Hill on the wagon road to Piute Creek and Fort Piute. Returning, hike up Piute Creek, but instead of following the wagon road over the hill, stay in the creek bed. As you pass above the point where water comes out of the ground, it becomes a dry canyon of spectacular proportions and great and colorful beauty. Follow that canyon completely through the mountain range, coming out via the gorge, near where your car is parked. In the old days, if travelers were using only riding horses or pack animals, they went through the gorge to avoid the climb up this hill.

66.

.4   But if they had wagons, they had to climb the hill
because there are places in the canyon where wagons
could not get through. Along the side of the gorge,
you can still see and follow the trace of the old pack
trail where it climbed out of the gorge, and that might
be a convenient point at which to park your vehicle.
This is an extensive hike. An entire day can be spent
at it. At least six hours should be allowed for the
complete loop.

You are treated to a wonderful view from the top
of Piute Hill. The great plain stretching out before you
and inclining upward to the west and north is Lanfair
Valley. The name Lanfair is taken from the name of an
early homesteader, Ernest L. Lanfair, who had a home
and settlement in the middle of the valley. We'll pass
near it later and say more about it. You are on the
edge of the vast Joshua tree forest that covers Lanfair
Valley and extends far beyond. In fact, it is a more
extensive Joshua tree forest than the one that gives
Joshua Tree National Monument its name. .

To the north 15 miles are the Castle Mountains, at
the southwestern base of which is the site of the old
mining town of Hart. To the northwest, on the horizon
20 miles away, are the beautiful and lofty New York
Mountains, which, with the Providence Mountains to the
south, form the backbone of the elevated country of the
East Mojave. Due west and extending just a little north
is the Mid Hills Region, and at a distance of 20 miles is
Rock Spring, the next stopping place on the Mojave
Road. There is a tiny notch in the horizon that marks
the site of Rock Spring. If you can locate that, you'll
see the trace of the Mojave Road here and there mean-
dering across the valley heading toward it. In wagon
road days, travelers on the Mojave Road knew about
that notch and used it to keep them from going astray
as they crossed this extensive plain. In line with the
Rock Spring notch, but in the foreground at a distance
of about 11 miles, you'll see a small white building
standing out in the midst of the Joshua tree forest.
You might need binoculars to see it. This is an Omni
Navigation site that aircraft use to help Guide them
across the country. If you spot it from Piute Hill, it
can help you identify the Rock Spring notch; and if
you can locate the Rock Spring notch, then you'll be
able to watch it in the distance as you cross Lanfair
Valley as the pioneers did. The Rock Spring notch is
just a little to the left of the Omni Station, and Rock
Spring is almost ten miles farther than the Omni

31.4 Station. As you approach Rock Spring you'll discover that the "Rock Spring Notch" is not really a notch in the hills. It's formed by the slopes of two hills approximately a mile apart, but from Piute Hill and when crossing most of Lanfair Valley this displacement is not discernible.

Due west from the top of Piute Mountain you can see Table Top Mountain at a distance of a little more than 20 miles (in case you're having trouble getting oriented, remember Table Top is to the left of the Rock Spring Notch). To the south of Table Top Mountain are the Providence Mountains. The Vontrigger Hills are to the southwest of your position, at a distance of about ten miles.

CATTLE INDUSTRY IN THE EAST MOJAVE

For more than 50 miles across the heart of the East Mojave, beginning in Piute Valley and continuing on to the eastern shore of Soda Lake, the route of the Mojave Road passes through cattle country. The cattle industry out here had its beginnings in the 1860s when the first miners and soldiers to enter this country brought small droves of cattle and sheep for their own subsistence. Cattle ranching on a commercial scale commenced in the 1880s. The largest and most extensive of the East Mojave cattle outfits was the Rock Springs Land & Cattle Company. It was not incorporated under that name until 1894, but it traced its beginnings to 1888; hence its principal brand was the "88." Old timers referred to it as the "88 outfit" or the "Rock Springs outfit."

At its height, the Rock Springs Company ran more than 10,000 head of cattle over more than a million acres of land. It expanded to that extent under the capable and kindhearted management of Earle G. Greening, the "grand old man" of the East Mojave cattle business.

The key to the cattle business on the East Mojave was control of the water sources, and then subsequent development of those sources to open the range to grazing at places where water did not exist naturally. Greening gained control over the water in many places by outright purchase of 40 acre parcels from the Land Office (predecessor of BLM) using "National Forest Script." This script consisted of certificates issued to individuals who held private land within the boundaries of newly formed national forests. The script could be

68.

exchanged for like amounts of land anywhere on the public domain. Greening acquired a quantity of script, and used it to purchase small parcels of land in the East Mojave that controlled water. What the Rock Springs Company could not buy outright, it acquired through the time honored custom of "possession is nine points of the law," and they picked up the tenth point by hiring men with fast guns.

In the early days, prior to 1910, the cattle inter-ests shared the East Mojave with miners and railroad men. There was no conflict among them. Miners and railroaders could afford to pay for their beef and there was no competition for natural resources. The indus-tries were mutually beneficial and they were not in the least competitive.

Around 1910, parts of the East Mojave, principally in Lanfair Valley and westward toward Pinto and Round Valleys, were opened to homestead location. During the next ten years literally hundreds of people moved to the area and attempted dry farming, thereby acquiring title to tracts of desert land. These were fairly wet years. Crops of impressive yields could be and were raised. The homesteaders could not flourish or prosper, but they could hang on.

Near the beginning of this period, June 13, 1910 to be exact, Earle Greening died and his son Walter took over active operations of the ranch. Conflict between cattlemen and homesteaders was probably inevitable anyway, but in any case the younger Green-ing's temperament was not such as to lessen the possi-bilities. There is no profit in attempting to find fault in the conflicts that followed. Points can be made on both sides.

The cattle would get into the homesteaders' crops. They could ruin a years work in a few hours. Some homesteaders felt the cattlemen deliberately pulled their fences down and let the cattle in. Homesteaders, faced with privations because their crops were lost in this way, sometimes felt justified in harvesting a little Rock Springs' beef. So conflicts developed between some homesteaders and some cattlemen. The controversy alternately raged and smoldered for 20 years. It is an exciting chapter in the history of this magnificent cattle country.

In the early days of East Mojave cattle raising, the ranchers learned that the key to success was to develop water where it existed naturally, and then pipe or haul it to dry parts of the range, thereby greatly expanding

ROUND UP IN THE EAST MOJAVE
A yearling steer is held tightly by ropes on front and rear. Linda Overson burns in the brand. Tim Overson (top of head showing in shadows) performs the necessary castration. Darwin Overson looks on holding the can to collect the parts removed from the steer. It's all in a day's ride and a very necessary part of cattle raising on the Kessler Springs Ranch.

ROCK SPRINGS LAND & CATTLE COMPANY
At one time the "88" brand of the Rock Springs Land &
Cattle Company appeared on livestock and various
inanimate objects throughout the East Mojave. This
watering trough, displaying this famous brand, is at a
spring on the Cima Dome. 26 November 1977.
Dennis Casebier Photo

31.4   the total number of acres that could be used for grazing. Considerable labor was put into the development of water distribution systems. These have been upgraded several times over the decades, but basically the original systems are still in place and performing the function for which they were designed many years ago.

When passing through this cattle country, you will see isolated corrals and usually there'll be water tanks associated with them. Sometimes they'll have water depending upon whether or not this part of the range is being used; and if so, the amount of water may be regulated by a float. The original source of the water may be many miles away.

Whether a particular corral or water source appears to be in use or not, keep in mind that this system is an essential part of the cattle industry as it exists on the public lands of the East Mojave. Although most ranchers own some patented land, the great bulk of their grazing lands are leased from the Federal Government through the Bureau of Land Management. The ranchers pay for every mouthful of forage their cattle eat.

As you might expect, the ranchers are apprehensive when people pass through the range on which they have a lease for grazing rights. They have supported us in the development of the Mojave Road as a recreational trail. Ed Eldridge, then owner and operator of the vast OX Cattle Company, commented to us: "Cattlemen have been here for a long time, but that wagon road was here before any of us."

As you travel through cattle country, consider yourself to be a friend and ally to the cattlemen, and you'll find they'll return the compliment every time. Take care to do no damage to any of the range improvements: fences, water tanks, pipelines, or windmills. Camp a quarter of a mile or more away from water sources so the half-wild desert range cattle won't be afraid to come in and drink. Don't shoot in an area where cattle are grazing. Don't hesitate to stop and meet the ranchers. Report any irregularities to them or to BLM.

To continue west on the Mojave Road Recreation Trail, go back down Piute Hill and through the range fence gate the same way you came up and pick up the road log at Mile 31.4 where we left it.

31.4   You are back at the point where you intersected the Mojave Road after taking the detour over the Cable Road through the Piute Range. The road to the south

LANFAIR VALLEY

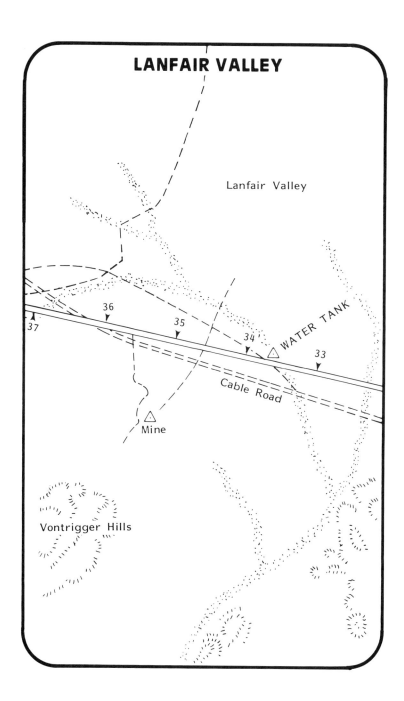

Lanfair Valley

36

35

34

WATER TANK

37

33

Cable Road

Mine

Vontrigger Hills

31.4 will take you back to the Cable Road (at the cattle guard) in 0.5 miles. To the north 0.3 miles is the Piute Corral. The corral may look old and abandoned. In fact, it is old, but it isn't abandoned. It is used from time to time by the OX Cattle Company when cattle are run on this part of the range. It is a wonderful and very colorful old corral. It can be photographed, studied, and admired; but on two counts it should not be disturbed in the least: first, it is the property of the cattle company; second, it is a valuable artifact. You'll see a number of corrals like this one as we cross the East Mojave. From the corral, it is 0.6 miles north to the trail head down into Piute Gorge. Now, head on west over the Mojave Road. (0.6).

32.0 You come to the edge of the ancient dry lake bed, an area that has little vegetation. (0.2).

32.2 Cross large wash. There are mesquites in the wash heavily burdened with mistletoe. It is not uncommon to see large hawks resting in the taller brush along washes like this one. They'll be there watching for their next meal. Mostly they'll be red-tailed hawks. Shooting them will do nobody any good. Nature can take care of the number of hawks very easily. Certainly it will be more uplifting for you personally to watch one of these magnificent creatures soar on the desert thermals, or to see one at close hand with the sun highlighting its red tail, than it will be for you to hold its limp and bloody body for a brief moment in your hands. The thrill of seeing one is a moment to be remembered and cherished, to kill one produces nothing but remorse. The vegetation here is still limited to creosote bushes and a few scattered yuccas. There are mesquite and catclaw bushes along the washes. (1.1).

33.3 Several faint roads lead to the north and at least one to the south, just before you reach the large wash at this point. Don't take any of these. (0.1).

33.4 Here is a large wash approximately 100 feet wide that drains a large section of Lanfair Valley. It is broad and sandy. There are cairns on both sides with a water tank visible to the west. After crossing the wash, the Mojave Road parallels it on the west side and heads north toward the large metal water tank. (0.3).

33.7 Intersection with well-traveled and well-maintained road. In fact, as you move toward the water tank, you actually drive on this improved road for 100 to 200 feet. If you follow this good road to the left (south), it'll take you to the Cable Road in 0.5 miles. To the north, it'll take you out into the heart of Lanfair Valley. (0.1).

.8   The Mojave Road, quite faint but marked by cairns, leads off to the left of the improved road. This is exactly opposite the large water tank. Make sure you have the correct route here before proceeding. There are enough roads in this vicinity to make it confusing. Remember, if you find yourself driving on a good road, you're on the wrong one! Go back to the water tank and hunt for cairns. (0.5).

.3   This is a scenic stretch of wagon road in pristine condition. It twists and turns quite a lot, and it must be driven slowly. But basically it isn't rocky. The stands of yucca and creosote bushes are increasing. (0.4).

.7   Intersection with a fairly new road that goes southwest 0.1 miles to the Cable Road, and northeast 0.2 miles to intersect with the good road that passed by the water tank at Mile 33.8. (0.1).

.8   The first Joshua trees appear. They will be widely scattered at first but will increase in density as we go west and gain altitude on the trek toward Rock Spring. Although there are a few stretches where you come out of the Joshua tree forest, you will be passing through scenery adorned by this beautiful and mystical desert plant until about Mile 77. (0.6).

.4   Road twists down to cross a small wash. (0.3).

.7   Again, the road twists down to cross a wash at a fairly shallow angle. If flooding has occurred since the pass-ing of vehicles, care must be exercised to pick up the trail on the opposite side of the wash. (0.4).

1   Intersection with the Cable Road. The Mojave Road crosses at a shallow angle, and it is fairly faint here. If you suddenly find yourself driving on an improved road, then you've been pulled off on the Cable Road, and you'd better go back and try again. (0.7).

8   To this point from the Cable Road intersection, the Mojave Road is in excellent wagon road condition. Here you drop into a large wash. (0.1).

9   Middle of a large wash. The bank is steeper on the east than on the west. After flooding or lack of use, the road can be difficult to follow to the west. (0.4).

3   Beyond the wash, we enter an area that was cleared during the homestead period. Vegetation was all re-moved and not much has come back. People have lived here during recent years. Note the remains of an old bus off to the right. The Mojave Road is reduced to only a faint trench in places. You actually drive off to the left (south) adjacent to the last remaining traces of the old road. (0.2).

37.5   Intersection of three roads. The Mojave Road is the northerly road of the two roads that head generally west. It is marked by two cairns and two Joshua trees on the north side of the road. The faint trace of a road heading slightly south of west is a pipeline road. The road heading east reaches the Cable Road in 0.6 miles. The road north goes 0.4 miles to the Cable Road, while south it goes 2.0 miles to an intersection, where a turn west for an additional 2.4 miles brings you to the Ivanpah-Goffs Road at a point about 2 miles south of Lanfair.

        This intersection is a good spot to get oriented in the Lanfair Valley area. Looking up the northbound road, the Hart mining area with its light colored clay mine tailings are visible slightly to the right, about 15 miles away, while the Castle Buttes are slightly to the left. To the northwest are the "Grotto" Hills, in the foreground about seven miles off. Beyond the "Grotto" Hills on the horizon are the New York Mountains, Cedar Canyon is due west. West and slightly south, Table Top Mountain is clearly visible, with the Providence Mountains a little south of it and in the background. To the southwest are the Woods Mountains, and due south are the Vontrigger Hills. Along the eastern horizon is the Piute Range that we crossed earlier. There are two gaps visible in the Piute Range. The one due east is Piute Gorge, and the one to the south of that is the gap through which the Cable Road passes. Between these two gaps is a small low, pointed peak; the Mojave Road passes over the Piute Range just south of this small peak.

        We placed the name "Grotto" in quotes because that is the wrong spelling for the name of these hills. Unfortunately the spelling "Grotto" is used on most modern maps. The name is derived from the surname of a homesteader named Mary Ann (King) Guirado, whose homestead was at the foot of these hills. Henceforth we shall refer to this prominent Lanfair Valley feature as the "Guirado Hills," in honor of the homesteader for which it was originally named. (0.6).

38.1   At this point the Mojave Road strikes an improved north-south road, and on the other side of it the way is blocked by a fence enclosing private land. A detour is required. Turn to the right (north) on this improved road for a distance of a little more than 0.2 miles. You'll come to an intersection with a maintained east-west road. There is a metal U. S. General Land Office survey marker at this corner dated 1920. Turn

76.

INDIAN HILL

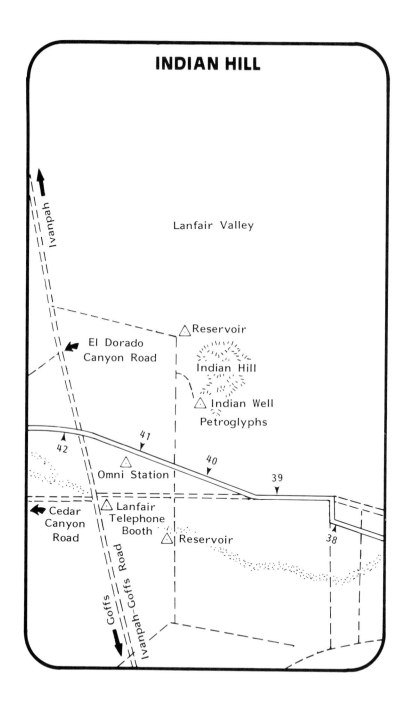

Lanfair Valley

△ Reservoir

Indian Hill

El Dorado
Canyon Road

Ivanpah

△ Indian Well

Petroglyphs

41

42

40

39

△ Omni Station

Cedar
Canyon
Road

△ Lanfair
Telephone
Booth

△ Reservoir

38

Goffs Road

Ivanpah–Goffs Road

38.1   left on a good road and proceed a little over 1.0 miles. Here the Mojave Road comes out from behind the fence, and there is no further obstruction. (1.2).

39.3   The Mojave Road angles off to the right here. The road is fairly faint and the angle is shallow. There are two large cairns to assist you in finding the right spot. But still you might have to hunt for it. WARNING!!! From this point westward to Mile 48.9 we encounter some of the roughest stretches of the Mojave Road Recreational Trail. The soil is generally firm -- although it can be muddy after it rains and it is sandy where the washes are crossed. It is quite rough. In places the old road is eroded into a deep and quite narrow ditch. It can be difficult driving for wide or long wheelbase vehicles. The various maps show that you can take the Cedar Canyon Road from this point to Mile 48.9 and avoid this stretch if you wish. The Cedar Canyon Road provides a quicker and smoother trip but you will miss some of the most beautiful and park-like Joshua tree forests that exist anywhere. It's a trade-off you'll have to evaluate. This is one of those places where it is particularly reckless to make the attempt if you are driving alone. There are a number of ways to get stuck during the next 8.5 miles and along most of the stretch you are removed from other roads and hence it would be difficult to get help if you did have trouble. Also cholla cactus are very thick in places in this same stretch, coming very close to the road. Take care not to hit them. The spines can work their way into your tires and you'll have a flat fifty miles down the road and never know why! (0.1).

39.4   Some places are quite rough, essentially like driving across open country. (0.7).

40.1   Cross Cable Road. The service road here is not nearly as well-maintained as before. It is no longer a graded high-speed road. The rut of the old road is a little to the left of the track presently being used by vehicles. (0.3).

40.4   Mojave Road is very deeply eroded into the form of a ditch. Caution and patience are required to navigate this stretch successfully. (0.2).

40.6   Junction with road to Indian Hill. This (the hill to your right) is called Indian Mountain by some old-timers. Others call it Indian Hill or Eagle Mountain. It is shown on the U.S.G.S. Lanfair Valley Quadrangle as Lanfair Buttes. To visit Indian Well (some call it Eagle Well) go north on this road 1.2 miles. There's a well traveled road at that point going hard right. Follow it for 0.3

6   miles. It'll take you into a little wash against the side of Indian Hill. Dark volcanic rock is the predominant feature there. There are petroglyphs on the rocks that rise up immediately adjacent to the road. At an angle at the foot of the cliff is Indian Well, an open shaft approximately 20 feet deep, with water at the bottom. It is dangerous. The rim is slippery, and care should be taken, particularly with children. The well is believed by some to be prehistoric. Others doubt that. Judge Edward J. Guirado, who, when he was a boy, moved to Lanfair Valley with his homesteader family, has told me he was present when the well was dug in 1911 or 1912 by Dan and Bert Webster. It is possible that there was some kind of excavation there previously and that the Websters enlarged or improved it, but in any case Edward Guirado was there when they worked on it. Edward and some others left their names and initials on the rocks there along with the date. Leave all the rocks undisturbed.

     Returning to the intersection between the Mojave Road and the Indian Hill Road, it can be noted that 0.3 miles to the south would take you back to the good graded road that runs directly west to Lanfair. To continue your journey of the Mojave Road, go directly across Indian Hill Road.(0.2).

8   Just west of the Indian Hill Road you'll notice a field with very little vegetation. During the homestead period many rectangular plots of land like this were cleared in Lanfair Valley. It was one of the requirements for proving up and gaining patent to the land. Most of it was done more than 60 years ago, and native vegetation is only slowly returning. Where the route of the Mojave Road crossed these plots, it was in some cases plowed under, but still the line of the old trail can generally be followed. In any case, the fields tend to be only about an eighth of a mile across, and the better defined sections of the trail are easily visible beyond them. (0.5).

3   As you drive along here, you'll notice a small white building with a peak on the top off to your left (south) less than an eighth of a mile distant. This is the "Omni Navigation Station" seen from the top of Piute Hill. It is the Goffs VOR station (VOR standing for Very High Frequency Omnidirectional Radio). It broadcasts its navigational signal, which consists simply of a taped voice identifying the station over and over, on a frequency of 114.4 Megahertz. This station, and others like it, is a key factor in flying by IFR (Instrument

PENNY CAN ON THE MOJAVE ROAD
With Spence Murray at the wheel, John Lawlor deposits
the traditional penny in the "Penny Can" at Mile 41.5.
October 26, 1983.

Jim Brokaw Photo

LANFAIR TELEPHONE BOOTH
Jean Lord places a call at the only telephone in this part of the world, situated at Lanfair, 0.8 miles south of the intersection between the Mojave Road and the Ivanpah-Goffs Road (Mile 41.9). April 1982.
Paul Lord Photo

41.3   Flight Rules) and is also used by many pilots flying VFR (Visual Flight Rules). (0.2).

41.5   There is a Joshua tree with limbs extending out over the old trail. There's a beer can hanging from one of the limbs, fastened by a wire. It is traditional to deposit a penny in the can as you pass. Add another can if the one is too full. (0.1).

41.6   Old road continues as a fairly good trace. There will be heavy stands of cholla cactus for the next six miles. Keep children and pets away from these patches. Also avoid running over the chollas or even brushing them with the sides of your tires. Cholla spines can cause both slow and fast tire leaks, sometimes months later. (0.3).

41.9   Intersection with Ivanpah-Goffs Road, sometimes called Lanfair Road. It is a high-speed, well-maintained county road that connects Goffs on the south (17.4 miles) with Ivanpah on the north (19.1 miles). It is 0.8 miles south to the site of Lanfair, a town during the homestead and railroad period. Now a telephone booth (with an operational telephone) there marks the junction of the Cedar Canyon Road with the Ivanpah-Goffs Road.

The Goffs General Store, which is at the intersection of "Old 66" and the main line of the Santa Fe Railroad, is particularly well suited to serve the needs of desert travelers. Their hours are roughly eight to eight, seven days a week. They have never been without gasoline -- at least for so many years that nobody can remember when there was a problem. They generally carry unleaded and regular gasoline. Water is available. A variety of refreshments is available, including a fair selection of canned goods that campers can use to augment the supplies they brought along. Frequently they have ice.

No services are available in Ivanpah, but there are services at Mountain Pass on I-15, which is 18 miles on beyond Ivanpah. Nipton is another desert community about 16 miles beyond Ivanpah. Nipton is an up-and-coming town featuring a general store, Nipton Mercantile, a restaurant, and other enterprises. There is water available. Gasoline is expected to be available there in the not-too-distant future.

Immediately adjacent to the Ivanpah-Goffs Road on the west side you go over a hump or berm. This is what is left of the roadbed of the old Nevada Southern Railroad. This colorful desert shortline -- first called Nevada Southern, then the California Eastern, and finally the Searchlight Branch of the Santa Fe -- was

LANFAIR STORE AND POST OFFICE
A 1921 view of Ned Farmer's store and post office in
Lanfair. Along with Maruba, Lanfair served as the
"civic center" of the large homesteader population that
lived in the Lanfair Valley region 1910-1925.
Wilma Buchen Krause Collection

TAKING LANFAIR VALLEY PRODUCE TO MARKET
Lee Buchen and Sherman Wilhelm at Millard Elliott's
homestead loading melons for delivery to the Needles
market. About 1921.
Wilma Buchen Krause Collection

PINTO VALLEY MELONS
Ida and Billy Gladwill pose with melons raised on their
homestead in Pinto Valley area. Pinto Mountain
dominates the horizon immediately behind Billy.
Wilma Buchen Krause Collection

41.9   originally built to connect mines in this part of the
         California and Nevada desert country with the mill and
         smelter at Needles. The road commenced at Goffs, then
         called Blake, on the Santa Fe main line, and ran 29.6
         miles up to Barnwell, then called Manvel, in the New
         York Mountains. (The site of Barnwell is about 10.2
         miles north of here.) Construction commenced in
         January 1893, and by September of that year, trains
         were running to Barnwell. Later the line was extended
         another 15.6 miles through the mountains from
         Barnwell, via Vanderbilt and Leastalk at the Union
         Pacific Railroad, to a railhead at the south end of
         Ivanpah Dry Lake named (what else?) Ivanpah. This
         was intended to serve mines to the north as far as the
         original Ivanpah in the Clark Mountains. When the
         northern end of the line beyond the crossing was
         abandoned, Leastalk took the name of Ivanpah, the
         third and present site to bear that name. Possibly the
         reason for the persistent use of this name was that the
         first Ivanpah was one of the original goals of the line.
         In 1907 a branch was run 22.6 miles eastward from
         Barnwell to Searchlight, Nevada. Eventually the line
         from Goffs to Searchlight was taken over by the Santa
         Fe and it became known as "the Searchlight Branch of
         the Santa Fe."
              This was never a very lucrative railroad. It was a
         victim of the vagaries of desert mining booms. But
         there was business inducement enough in this country
         to keep it alive until 1923, and the railroad was a
         driving force in all three major activities that existed
         out here in those years: mining, the cattle industry,
         and homesteading. Trains hauled the miners' ore to the
         mills; they carried cattle to market and to feedlots; and
         they hauled emigrant cars for the homesteaders and
         provided them with supplies and transportation to the
         outside world once they were established.
              In addition to financial difficulties arising from
         insufficient business, this line suffered loss after loss
         resulting from washouts along the track. Heavy flooding
         in 1923 made it impractical to rebuild, so the railroad
         was abandoned in that year and the track was taken
         up. The local people -- miners, cattlemen, and home-
         steaders -- lost no time in appropriating the ties and
         bridge timbers. You'll notice they were used in the
         construction of many of the older buildings and corrals
         in this country. This was the last contribution of the
         old Nevada Southern to the welfare of the residents of
         the East Mojave.

MAJOR WAGON ROAD INTERSECTION
At Mile 43.6 a road takes off to the northeast. This was the El Dorado Canyon Road. Travelers headed east took that route if their destination was Utah, while those headed for Arizona continued on the Mojave Road. This was a major intersection in the 1860s. October 13, 1975.
Dennis Casebier Photo

41.9   The railroad sidings nearest to where you are situated now were Lanfair, 0.8 miles to the south, and Ledge (also known as Maruba), 2.7 miles to the north, where the OX Cattle Company Headquarters are today. (0.0+).

41.9+   West of the Ivanpah-Goffs Road is a heavy stand of extremely large chollas, some of them as high as a vehicle. As you proceed west, heavy stands of vegetation, predominated by Joshua trees and chollas, continue on to the Guirado Hills Primitive Campsite Road. This region is beautiful, having an almost park-like appearance. (0.8).

42.7   Cross large wash. This is the wash that runs along the southwestern side of Guirado Hills and borders the primitive camp site. (0.9).

43.6   Junction of the Mojave Road and the El Dorado Canyon Road. El Dorado Canyon is usually a dry side canyon coming in to the Colorado River from the west about 25 miles below Hoover Dam, in the present state of Nevada. It is the site of the earliest mining activity in the East Mojave Desert region. Prospectors and miners were at work there at least as early as 1861. Their route to the mines from Los Angeles took the Mojave Road to this point. From here the El Dorado Canyon Road angled off to the northeast via Lewis Holes toward the present Searchlight, Nevada, then turned northward to El Dorado Canyon. Connections were developed from El Dorado Canyon to Las Vegas and the main Salt Lake Trail. Hence, a traveler from the Los Angeles area could reach Las Vegas and Utah by way of the Mojave Road and the El Dorado Canyon Road, and during the 1860s and 1870s many travelers did go that way. This point was a major road junction in its day. Here travelers had to decide whether to go northeast toward Utah or continue directly east on the Mojave Road toward Arizona and New Mexico. In that sense, this intersection fulfilled the same purpose as the present junction of I-15 and I-40 in Barstow. (0.2).

43.8   Intersection with the north-south road that runs from the Cedar Canyon Road to Guirado Hills Primitive Camp Site. It is 0.8 miles south to the Cedar Canyon Road or 1.2 miles north to the camp site. There are no improvements or facilities at this camp site. It is simply one of the many places where people traveling the Mojave Road sometimes camp. Frequently, depending upon how much time is available to drive the trail, travelers may find it convenient to camp here the first night out from the Colorado River. There is a fire circle at the site (just a

88.

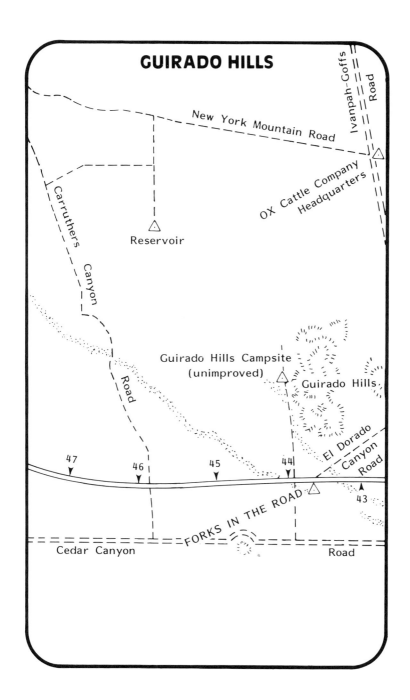

GUIRADO HILLS

Ivanpah-Goffs Road

New York Mountain Road

OX Cattle Company Headquarters

Carruthers Canyon

Reservoir

Road

Guirado Hills Campsite
(unimproved)

Guirado Hills

El Dorado Canyon Road

47   46   45   44   43

FORKS IN THE ROAD

Cedar Canyon   Road

MOJAVE ROAD CARAVAN IN LANFAIR VALLEY
A caravan takes a break on a rough stretch of the trail
in Lanfair Valley at about Mile 44. March 3, 1983.
Dennis Casebier Photo

MOJAVE ROAD
Some stretches of the Mojave Road in Lanfair Valley have become deeply eroded as part of the local drainage system. Smaller vehicles negotiate these stretches more gracefully than larger vehicles (Mile 47.3). December 27, 1982.

Dennis Casebier Photo

INTERSECTION WITH CARRUTHERS CANYON ROAD
Dennis Casebier and Spence Murray on the Mojave Road at the intersection with the Carruthers Canyon Road (Mile 45.9). March 6, 1982.
Jim Crow Photo

.8   few local stones arranged into a ring), but it is neces-
     sary for you to bring your own wood. (0.1).

.9   Cross large wash with steep bank on west side. Road
     continues straight across. (0.1).

.0   Heavy stands of cholla. Good view of New York Moun-
     tains to the right (north). (0.7).

.7   Road becomes a ditch, forming part of the local drain-
     age system. Some drivers will want to travel to the left
     (south) of the ditch. There is a fairly steep rise get-
     ting up to the south side. It is not necessary to be up
     out of the ditch more than about 0.1 miles. (0.3).

.0   Road becomes quite sandy. (0.9).

.9   Intersection with Carruthers Canyon Road. To the
     north it is about 7.5 miles to the mouth of Carruthers
     Canyon. Just a short way northwest from this intersec-
     tion is a stone house. It is not abandoned, and should
     not be approached nor disturbed in any way.

         Carruthers Canyon penetrates the New York
     Mountain range. There are delightful elevated camping
     places there that are high enough to be comfortable
     even in the heat of summer. These are among piñon
     trees and in a canyon with magnificent granite
     outcrops. There has been mining activity in this canyon
     and, in fact, some of the earliest mining activity in the
     East Mojave took place in and around Carruthers
     Canyon in the 1860s. (0.4).

.3   Wash with fairly bad drop-off. (0.4).

.7   Road becomes a ditch again with loose sandy bottom.
     Driving should be quite slow. Without a breeze more
     dust enters the vehicle than before, accompanied by a
     mixture of pleasant odors, mostly originating with the
     various species of desert plants you are passing
     through. (0.2).

.9   We emerge from the thick forest of Joshua trees and
     other vegetation and break into a cleared field. At this
     point, the Cedar Canyon Road is approximately 100
     yards to the south, and we'll parallel it until we cross
     it at Mile 48.9. This cleared field is less than a quarter
     of a mile across. The road is faint where it crosses.

         At this point you are just entering Section 6 T12N
     R16E. The E 1/2 of that section, roughly spanned by
     our Mile 47.9 to Mile 48.4 was homesteaded by Lewis
     Emde on November 29, 1912. He received patent to the
     land on May 3, 1921. This is the same man for whom
     Emde Well near Rock Spring is named. (0.2).

.1   Western edge of the cleared field. The remains of
     homestead improvements are visible as you cross the
     field. (0.3).

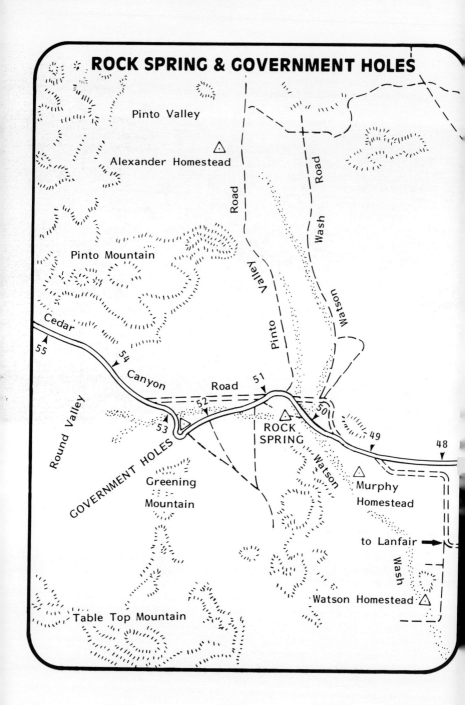

ROCK SPRING & GOVERNMENT HOLES

Pinto Valley

Alexander Homestead

Pinto Mountain

Pinto Valley Road

Wash Road

Watson

Cedar

55

54

Canyon

Road

51

52

53

50

49

48

Round Valley

GOVERNMENT HOLES

ROCK SPRING

Watson

Greening

Mountain

Murphy
Homestead

to Lanfair

Wash

Watson Homestead

Table Top Mountain

94.

DESCENDING INTO WATSON WASH

This is the point at which the Mojave Road Recreation
Trail drops into Watson Wash. (Watson Wash is named
for Lorenzo and Harriet Watson and their family who
homesteaded near here in 1914.) It is a short, but
steep, descent. In the old days there were two routes
taken down into the wash. The other was to the north
directly across from Rock Spring Canyon.

Dennis Casebier Photo

48.4   Large pancake cactus off to the right. These grow also at Rock Spring, but they appear in very few other places in the East Mojave. (0.1).

48.5   Intersection with the Cable Road, which at this point is badly eroded and rarely traveled, probably because of the proximity of the Cedar Canyon Road which can be utilized as an access road. The Mojave Road crosses the Cable Road at a fairly shallow angle. Be sure not to proceed up the wrong road! (0.0+).

48.5+   After passing the Cable Road, the trace of the Mojave Road is a groove or ditch. It looks more like a wash of some kind rather than like an old road. Rough. (0.4).

48.9   The Mojave Road strikes the Cedar Canyon road. It then follows that road for 0.4 miles west, after which the Mojave Road angles off to the left. (0.4).

49.3   Turn left (shallow angle) off Cedar Canyon Road. Exit is marked by cairns. (0.2).

49.5   This is the point at which the Mojave Road drops down into Watson Wash. It is quite a steep little hill. Some road work was done here to render the descent somewhat more graceful. But the condition of the road here could vary considerably following rainstorms, which can reach impressive proportions in this vicinity. We built quite a large cairn at this point so it would be visible from the Cedar Canyon Road. Once down the hill you angle northwest up Watson Wash toward Rock Spring. We have put cairns across this wash showing the way, but, of course, they could get washed away. Keep in mind that Watson and Rock Spring washes can both be extremely dangerous in time of flood. Watson Wash drains much of Pinto Valley, and Rock Spring Wash drains much of Round Valley. Because these are elevated valleys surrounded by even higher mountains, extremely heavy rains can fall in relatively short intervals causing dangerous flash floods. It would be extremely reckless to camp overnight in either of these washes at any time. (0.2).

49.7   Once down off the ridge and into Watson Wash at this mileage, head up the wash crossing it diagonally to the left toward the mouth of Rock Spring Canyon. (0.4).

50.1   You are at the intersection of the larger Watson Wash and the mouth of Rock Spring Canyon which comes in on the west side of Watson Wash. Bear left and proceed up Rock Spring Canyon. (0.2).

50.3   When you drive westerly up the sandy wash as far as you can go (you'll be stopped by rocks) you are within a few feet of Rock Spring. You may park here or you may go back the way you came a short distance to the

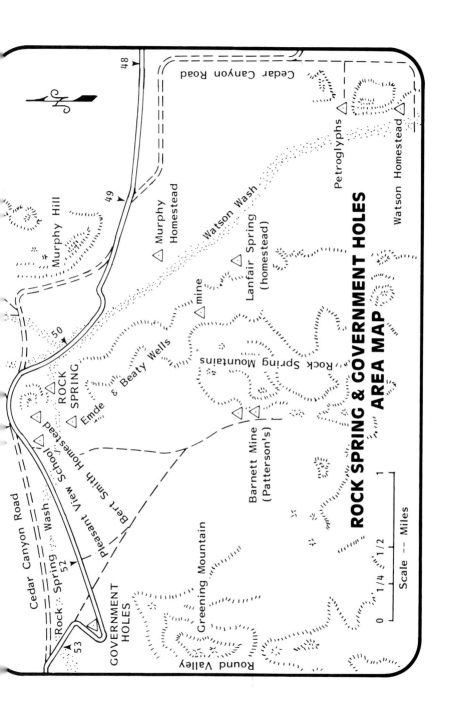

ROCK SPRING & GOVERNMENT HOLES
AREA MAP

Cedar Canyon Road

48

49

Murphy Hill

Murphy Homestead

50

ROCK SPRING

Emde & Beaty Wells

mine

Watson Wash

Lanfair Spring (homestead)

Rock Spring Mountains

Petroglyphs

Watson Homestead

Pleasant View School

Bert Smith Homestead

Rock Spring Wash

Cedar Canyon Road

52

Barnett Mine (Patterson's)

Greening Mountain

53

GOVERNMENT HOLES

Round Valley

Scale -- Miles

0   1/4   1/2   1

97.

50.3   improved parking lot. In this narrative we'll assume you drive on to the improved parking lot. At the spring you reverse your direction and drive back down the wash 0.15 miles to the intersection between Rock Spring Wash and Watson Wash and bear around to the left and follow the road that goes up to the cleared parking area on the northwest intersection of the washes. (0.2).

50.5   At the parking area there is a post and cable barricade to prevent driving on the site of old Camp Rock Spring, and a bulletin board, all erected by BLM. If you've found these improvements, you can be sure you've found the right spot.

Rock Spring is situated just beyond the eastern edge of Round Valley in the Mid Hills Region of the Providence Mountains. The spring occurs in a wash that passes through a mountain spur. In the canyon the bed of the wash is solid granite strewn with large granite boulders. Above and below this short canyon (about one quarter mile), the wash is sandy with shallow banks. The wash drains much of Round Valley. When heavy rains fall in Round Valley, violent flash floods come down this wash and roar through Rock Spring Canyon, further polishing the rocks and sometimes raising or lowering the level of the sand below the canyon.

The spring or seeps of water occur at the lower or eastern end of Rock Spring Canyon. Water rises at several places through cracks in the rock and builds into a small stream which runs for only a short distance (commonly not more than 30 or 40 yards and frequently much less) and then sinks into the sand. The amount of water issuing from these seeps varies considerably depending upon the amount of rain that has fallen in Round Valley in recent months. At times in the past, there has been enough water there for homesteader children to use as swimming holes. At other times, the amount of water available would not contain enough to fill an ordinary tub. In lush times, a stream is formed and water gurgles over the rocks. In drier times, the water barely moves and is impregnated everywhere with moss and algae. Bees and other insects swarm around the small surface area to collect the life-giving water.

A few hundred yards below Rock Spring, the wash joins Watson Wash, the main wash from Pinto Valley, and turns south. On the north side of Rock Spring Wash just below the canyon mouth, there is a little shelf of land elevated a few feet above the wash. This small spot (less than five acres) is sheltered by the

ROCK SPRING

At Rock Spring, water seeps up through cracks in granite rock. Except for short periods after rainstorms, it is always a small flow. After long periods without rain in Round Valley, the spring disappears altogether.

Dennis Casebier Photo

LEVI H. ROBINSON
Robinson commanded Camp Rock Spring during part of
1867 as a lieutenant in the 14th U. S. Infantry.
Library of Congress Collections

100.

mountain spur through which Rock Spring Canyon passes. In earlier times it provided protection to Indians and later white men from prevailing winds from the west. This was an important factor where the elevation is near 5,000 feet, and ice frequently forms to a depth of one or more inches overnight in the winter.

One of the most prominent mountain ranges in the Eastern Mojave Desert is the Providence and New York Mountain chain. In the old days this entire chain was referred to as the Providence Mountains. In approximately the middle of this system of mountains there is a natural pass. The mountains are lower here, and there is a break provided by washes and shallow canyons, allowing access from one side of the range to the other. This is the Mid Hills Region. The mountains are approached from the Lanfair Valley on the east by way of Rock Spring. The natural passage through the mountains goes across Round Valley and then heads on westward out of the mountains by way of Cedar Canyon.

Rock Spring owes its historical importance to its strategic location in this pass through the Providence Mountains. In crossing the East Mojave in an east-west direction over countless years of prehistory, the Indians used this pass and, of course, they used the water at Rock Spring. When white men began to arrive, the Indians showed them the way. Their trail, and later wagon road, followed a chain of springs across the Eastern Mojave connecting the Mojave Indian villages on the Colorado River on the east with the sink of the Mojave River on the west. Rock Spring was a vital link in this chain. Most early travelers went that way. They used the water at Rock Spring, and camped on that little shelf of land below the spring. Throughout much of the earlier periods, there were no man-made structures here. The site was about as empty and deserted-looking as it is today.

Over a period of years a number of structures were erected on the little shelf below the springs. Very little of them remains today. There are a few foundations, rows of rocks, and the visible signs of a dugout or fallen tunnel; but for the most part, the structures are gone.

But the setting is the same. The scenery around Rock Spring is not very different today from what it was before the white men came. The preserved natural integrity of the immediate site and the surrounding country is one of its most important qualities.

ROCK SPRING IN 1863-1864

A photographer named Rudolph d'Heureuse took this historic photograph at Rock Spring in 1863 or 1864. Compare with the picture on the facing page taken in 1980. It can be seen the floor of the wash is much lower now than it was in the 1860s. The level of the wash seems to be a function of the intensity of the most recent flash flood.

University of California, Berkeley
Bancroft Library Collections

ROCK SPRING IN 1980

This is a contingent of the group that participated in
the First Mojave Road Rendezvous in November of 1980.
They are posed in Rock Spring Wash and the
photographer has stationed himself in the exact spot
used by Rudolph d'Heureuse to take his famous
photograph in 1863-1864.

Dennis Casebier Photo

50.5   Above Rock Spring, World War I Veteran Bert G.
Smith built a stone house in the early 1930s, and it is
still standing and currently occupied. But that cabin
and the remains of a few wells and dikes constructed at
Rock Spring Canyon in an effort to improve water
production are all that are left.

There is a county road (the Cedar Canyon Road)
that runs within about a quarter of a mile of the Rock
Spring site. From some points at the Rock Spring site,
this road is visible as is traffic going over it. But for
the most part the site is isolated from such visual
intrusions.

There are drawings and photographs of some of
the structures and improvements that existed at one
time at Rock Spring. It is not thought likely or desir-
able that any structures will be rebuilt or reconstructed
there but the history can be brought back to life with
the photographs and other artwork. One of the most
interesting of the early photos of Rock Spring is reproduced in this Guide so visitors will have the adventure
of finding where the photographer stood in 1863 or 1864
and seeing what changes have occurred in 120+ years.
In 1985, East Mojave artist Carl Faber created a
magnificent painting of that same scene, placing the
same historical figures in the painting that were in the
photograph. Carl lives in Bert Smith's cabin at Rock
Spring. (0.0).

TED JENSEN

104.

ROCK SPRING TO MARL SPRINGS

5   Leaving Rock Spring. On leaving the area it will be assumed you are in the parking lot in front of the barricade and bulletin board. Head north against the hill on the west side of Watson Wash (Drum Peak -- named for John Drum who commanded Camp Rock Spring during much of its existence -- is visible to the north on the horizon). (0.2).

7   Intersection with Cedar Canyon Road. Turn left or west. This is a major well-maintained county road. As you turn left the road climbs around the end of a hill. You'll stay on the Cedar Canyon Road here for only a short distance. (Distances from this intersection to points of interest by way of the Cedar Canyon Road are: west to Black Canyon Road 5.9 miles; west to Kelso-Cima Road [total distance] 12.2 miles; east to Lanfair 10.4 miles). (0.3).

0   Turn left off Cedar Canyon Road as you climb up the hill. This is a lesser road than the Cedar Canyon Road, but still a good road. (0.1).

1   Intersection with local road. Continue straight. To the left a driveway takes you to Bert Smith's old homestead and the road to the right takes you back to Cedar Canyon Road. Bert Smith's homestead is private property. For several years, and at the time of publication of this Guide, this residence is occupied by Carl Faber, famous East Mojave desert artist. (0.1).

2   Faint road to left (south) would take you to the site of the old Barnett or Patterson Mine. It's a rough road, very narrow and sandy in places. If you're concerned about the condition of the road and want to visit the Barnett Mine, take the road that goes to that point at Mile 52.2 instead of this one. Continue straight ahead now. (0.3).

    Road crosses the Rock Spring Wash. This should be approached slowly. The road is not maintained regularly. Depending upon the occurrence of flash floods, there can be a cliff on the near side of the wash. It can be quite sandy in crossing the wash and along the road beyond it. (0.0+).

+   There is a beautiful view of Pinto Mountain to the right. Greening Mountain, named for cattleman Earle G. Greening, is straight ahead. Round Valley is spread out before you. (0.5).

    Road to left goes to Barnett Mine. Poor road. (0.2).

    This road to the left is the best road to Barnett Mine. Road to right leads to Government Holes corral.

52.2   Continue straight ahead. The road you're on will go
        above Government Holes, and you'll be coming back
        down through the corral. (0.4).

52.6   You are at Government Holes, where there is a
        cottonwood tree, windmill, and water tank. As you have
        seen, Government Holes and Rock Spring are quite
        close together -- about two miles. They were both major
        points on the old wagon road. Rock Spring was the
        better camping spot, but the water supply sometimes
        failed. Government Holes is in a more exposed position,
        open to the ravages of weather at this high desert
        elevation, but the water supply was almost always
        reliable.

        The first well at Government Holes was dug by
        teamsters in the employee of Phineas Banning,
        Wilmington, California, merchant and forwarding agent
        and the man for whom Banning, California, was later
        named. They called their creation Banning's Well. The
        next year the well was enlarged by U. S. soldiers and
        it became known as Government Holes or, less often,
        Government Wells. Even though the plural "holes" is
        commonly used, it appears there is only one well and
        that there never was more than one.

        Countless early travelers on the Mojave Road
        camped at Government Holes and made use of its water.
        From a historical point of view, the most significant
        phase of Government Holes history was its role as an
        operations point for the cattle industry. This probably
        started as early as 1888 and it has continued down to
        the present time. (If you decide to camp near
        Government Holes, be sure you do so at least a quarter
        of a mile away so you won't interfere with cattle or
        wildlife.)

        The most famous incident in the history of Govern-
        ment Holes occurred on November 8, 1925, when two
        men shot it out in the cabin there. Both were killed.
        Their names were Matt Burts and J. W. "Bill" Robin-
        son. They were both vestiges of a chapter in western
        history that most thought had already passed. They
        were gunfighters. One worked for the cattle company
        and was used by them to protect their interests and the
        other had previously worked for the cattle company,
        but at the time in question, he was involved in various
        pursuits in Lanfair Valley.

        The cattle company had stationed Robinson at
        Government Holes. There had been talk in the Valley
        that Robinson had been hired to kill Burts and Bob
        Hollimon, another former gunfighter who was a source

GOVERNMENT HOLES

This photograph shows the building in which the gun fight took place between Matt Burts and J. W. "Bill" Robinson on November 8, 1925, when both men were killed.

Harold O. Weight Photo

Matt Burts
Betty Ordway Photo

52.6   of concern to the cattle company. It is felt by many
        that the immediate cause of the fight on November 8th
        was the gossip or talk that had gone on in the valley
        about these two men.
            On that day, a Sunday, Matt Burts arrived at
        Government Holes in a Model "T" in company with a
        Mrs. L. A. Riedell and her grandson H. L. or R. L.
        Fulton (spelling is different in different accounts).
        Robinson was in the cabin. Burts yelled into the cabin
        saying they needed water for the car. Robinson yelled
        back his acknowledgement and approval. Then he
        invited Burts inside while Mrs. Riedell and her grand-
        son tended to the car.
            Mrs. Riedell heard voices inside and then a terri-
        ble noise. The gunfighters had each emptied their .45s
        into one another. They were both dead or soon would
        be.
            After these few facts, the story becomes confused
        and contradictory. There is a hint that one of the
        bullets in Robinson came from a rifle. Burts had no
        rifle. Mrs. Riedell and her grandson were taken into
        custody by the San Bernardino County Sheriff and held
        for questioning for awhile, but soon released. The
        episode at Government Holes became part of the colorful
        history of the East Mojave. Doubtless it was one of the
        last classical gunfights of the old west.

52.6   Leaving Government Holes. Drive on diagonally through
        the corral, passing the old Rock Springs Land & Cattle
        Company circular concrete watering trough. Go out the
        north gate of the corral and bear left. (0.1).

52.7   Just outside the north gate a road goes off to the
        right. This intersects the road we came in on at Mile
        52.2. Continue ahead, bearing left. Soon our road dead
        ends into another road. Turn left. (0.3).

53.0   Cross Rock Spring Wash. (0.1).

53.1   Meet and join the Cedar Canyon Road. Turn left on
        Cedar Canyon Road. You'll be traveling on the Cedar
        Canyon Road for several miles. (0.3).

53.4   Cross over cattle guard. (1.4).

54.8   Cross second cattle guard. Pinto Mountain is the promi-
        nent feature to your right (north). Round Valley,
        bounded by Table Top Mountain on the southern end,
        is on your left (south). You are approaching the head
        of Cedar Canyon down which you'll soon be traveling.
        (0.0+).

54.8+   The stretch through Round Valley is the highest part
        of the Mojave Road -- about 5,000 feet. The air is
        usually extremely clear here in Round Valley, and the

8+ sky an intense blue. It is high enough that even in the heat of summer it is ordinarily not uncomfortable. Near the crest you encounter sagebrush, the dominate shrub that flourishes at this higher elevation. As you drop into Cedar Canyon you'll see thick growths of piñon and juniper. Joshua trees, that have been absent for a few miles, will reappear and be present along the road again for many miles. (1.5).

3 Shortly before reaching the intersection with the Black Canyon Road, there is a faint road going off to the right up a small canyon for a quarter of a mile or so. There is a spring in that canyon called Cedar Spring that was known and utilized by teamsters in wagon road days. Sometimes quite a stream flows over the rocks in that canyon, but after a period of drought, it is completely dry. (0.2).

5 Junction with the Black Canyon Road, a major, well-maintained county road that provides relatively high-speed access to the south as far as I-40. It is 18.1 miles south to where the road becomes black-topped, and a total of 27.8 miles to I-40. Mid Hills Campground, Hole-in-the-Wall Campground, and Mitchell Caverns are also reached by taking the Black Canyon Road to the south at this point. To follow the Mojave Road, continue on downhill on the Cedar Canyon Road. (1.0).

5 Generally speaking, you can travel the Cedar Canyon Road at fairly high speeds. But at this point, there is a rather sharp, blind, lefthand curve, which should be approached slowly and with caution. (0.1).

6 Along this stretch the old wagon road was in Cedar Canyon Wash, and not up here on the present Cedar Canyon Road. The purist may want to get down in the wash and drive through the canyon that way. Down a little farther there is a short stretch where traces of the old trail are visible on the north side of the wash. (1.0).

6 You've been traveling on the left or south side of Cedar Canyon Wash. At this point the road crosses the wash and then climbs out of the canyon altogether on the north side. The old wagon road climbed out at about the same place. Once you've climbed up out of the canyon, you are suddenly presented with one of the most magnificent vistas that exists anywhere in the East Mojave. Much of the geography of the East Mojave is spread out before you. It is worthwhile to drive until the Kelso Dunes come into view on your left; then stop and orient yourself.

CEDAR CANYON

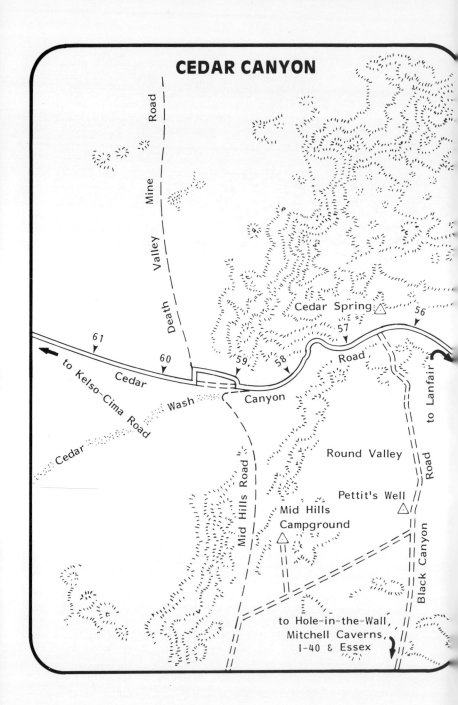

6

Off to the left you'll see the impressive Kelso Dunes; piles of sand there are more than 500 feet high. The town of Kelso is on the U.P.R.R. just this side of the dunes. Beyond the dunes are the imposing Granite Mountains. Beyond the Kelso Dunes to the right is the blow sand area known as the Devil's Playground. If the day is clear, you can even see the San Bernardino Mountains, frequently snow-covered, far off to the southwest. To your extreme left, continuing south from where you are, is the imposing western side of the Providence Mountains. Looking straight ahead, the smaller mountains in the foreground are the Beale Mountains, named for Edward Fitzgerald Beale, the explorer who brought camels to the East Mojave in the 1850s. Behind the Beale Mountains are the Marl Mountains, which will be the next stopping place on the Mojave Road (Marl Springs). The old wagon road itself can be seen wandering through the Joshua tree forest and passing around the north side of the Beale Mountains (don't confuse it with the straight road to the left which marks the line of the underground telephone cable). This is the best vista of a long stretch of pristine wagon road. If the day is clear and you've got a telephoto lens, interesting pictures of the wagon road can be taken here. Shifting to the right you can see Cimacito, which appears as a small, smooth, dome-shaped outline on the horizon, and, in that vicinity, a few cinder cones extend their heads in the distance. We'll be passing right by them later. To the right of the cinder cones is Cima Dome, that interesting geological feature shaped somewhat like an inverted gold pan approximately ten miles in diameter. Cima Dome is blessed with quite a number of good water sources and is covered with a luxuriant Joshua tree forest. It is one of the most beautiful natural areas in the East Mojave. The small volcanic outcrop on the right side of Cima Dome is Tuetonia Peak. To the right of Cima Dome are the Ivanpah Mountains. Sometimes the even more distant Clark Mountain can be seen above the Ivanpahs. Clark Mountain is the loftiest peak in the East Mojave (7,929 feet). On this side of the Ivanpahs is the town of Cima, located at the summit on the U.P.R.R. between Kelso and Ivanpah Valleys. (0.3).

Just after the Cedar Canyon Road climbs up out of Cedar Wash, the old Mojave Road takes off from the existing county road at a slight angle to the right (if you drove ahead a ways to see the vista described in the preceding entry, then you'll have to return to this

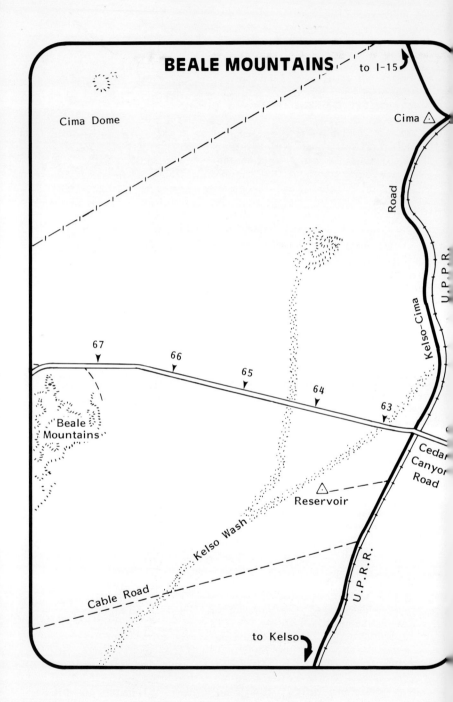

BEALE MOUNTAINS

to I-15

Cima Dome

Cima

Road

Kelso–Cima

U.P.R.

67

66

65

64

63

Beale
Mountains

Cedar
Canyon
Road

Reservoir

Kelso Wash

Cable Road

U.P.R.

to Kelso

CARTOONS by TED JENSEN

D. RATT
(or Deserti Rattus)

D. Ratt is a cartoon character created by Barstow artist Ted Jensen. D. Ratt is a desert rat in the most literal tradition -- he is also the mascot of the Friends of the Mojave Road. He was originally developed by Ted in 1980 to depict the adventures of Marines from the Marine Corps Logistics Base in Barstow as they traveled the Mojave Road. D. Ratt was involved in a humorous way in the adventures of the Marines on the trail. Shortly after that, the Friends of the Mojave Road was founded. D. Ratt shed his Marine Corps uniform and became a Friend of the Mojave Road. Meanwhile, he had acquired a number of cartoon friends, like Hardshell McTrek, and others. Finally, in response to popular demand, Ted created a female companion, "D.D.".

The pages that follow feature some of our favorite of Ted's wonderful cartoons. They are selected to answer some of the questions you might have about how to deal with the desert and how to prepare for a trip over the Mojave Road.

Ted Jensen

Desert animals have special adaptations to cope with the water problems on the desert. Tortoises carry an extra supply in their shells for use during the long dry spells. Do not pick them up because they'll lose their water and it could mean death for them in the future. For yourself, take plenty of water. If you have a breakdown and don't have water, it is a life-threatening problem immediately. If you have sufficient supplies of water, it's an entirely different problem. On the desert you should drink frequently and be sure children drink frequently. Water from desert springs and wells is generally not drinkable without purification.

It is imperative that your vehicle be in tiptop shape and with good tires -- including the spare -- before leaving home on a desert outing. Always carry an assortment of hand tools and take a spare fan belt, a tire-patching kit and (especially in summer) extra radiator coolant. Many frequent desert travelers have learned from bitter experience to always travel in the company of another vehicle, since the odds of both of them breaking down or becoming stuck are greatly reduced. You should carry a repair manual to your vehicle.

TED JENSEN

In the best tradition of the "Old West," BLM Rangers are here to keep the peace, but these modern Rangers do this and a whole lot more. In addition to their duty to protect public lands, resources, and developments, they have maps and can give you directions so you can find your way to points of interest or back home. They can provide emergency medical care or call for assistance if your vehicle breaks down. They can give you a push (or pull) if you get stuck, issue you a fire permit, find you if you are lost, and teach you about the desert. Rangers are here to maintain law and order, and they are here to help you enjoy your visit to the Public Lands.

TED JENSEN

The Joshua tree grows in many places in the East Mojave above about 3,000 feet. Being large and tree-like, it frequently dominates the scenery and forms the basis for much of the scenic beauty and unique charm of the region. As with many other desert plants, the Joshua trees have developed special adaptations to survive in the harsh desert environment. And, like so many others, they grow very slowly, many being over 100 years old. The Joshua trees are protected and should not be disturbed in any way. Many other desert plants are protected by law, and all the vegetation in the East Mojave should be protected and respected by recreational users. Don't drive over them, pull them out, or in any other way disturb them.

TED JENSEN

There are hundreds of miles of "existing" and "designated" roads and trails requiring 4WD in the desert. BLM manages this resource and can provide maps and information on the various routes. The Mojave Road Recreation Trail is a special 130-mile 4WD trail for which there is an interpretive guide. Rock cairns, placed on the right side of the trail headed west, show the way. These cairns were erected by the Friends of the Mojave Road. There are many such opportunities for volunteers to participate in development of the recreational resources of the desert. Contact BLM or any organized recreation user group.

TED JENSEN

The East Mojave is largely public land administered by
the Bureau of Land Management under a multiple-use
concept. Recreation, mining, and cattle grazing might
be going on in the same acreage simultaneously. It is
especially important that we take care not to interfere
in any way with the ranching process. Frequently the
cattle are half-wild and can easily be frightened away
from the few water sources. You shouldn't camp near
the water or corrals nor spend an extended period of
time in the immediate proximity (not more than 30 min).
Don't allow cattle to be "run" by your vehicle. Slow
down and give them the right of way. Don't discharge
firearms at all in the vicinity of cattle and
improvements. Don't use windmills or other water
facilities for target practice. These improvements are all
the property of the ranchers. If gates are closed, close
them behind you. If they are open, leave them open.

The potential for recreational use of the desert is almost unlimited. Each user must be constantly sensitive to the needs of the others. Many are involved with "passive" uses, like artists, photographers, and those simply seeking the peacefulness and solitude of the desert. Others are pursuing more active recreation, such as hunters, shooters, and 4WD enthusiasts. The multiple-use concept will only work if each user protects the interests of all other users with the same vigor with which he defends his own use. Think about that the next time you go to the desert and study the other fellow and his needs.

There is a great variety of wildlife in the East Mojave, although most forms are scarce. It is OK to "shoot" the wildlife, as long as you do it with a camera. It takes patience and perseverance to get good wildlife photos on the desert, but the results can be rewarding. For this purpose a 200MM lens is recommended. You can hand-hold a lens of that focal length, yet it is powerful enough to help get "close" to some of the shy or dangerous forms of desert wildlife. Be careful not to impact nesting sites or otherwise disturb the natural setting. Be careful photographing rattlesnakes or other potentially dangerous citizens of the desert.

A prospector ghost from the past lures D. Ratt into an abandoned mine tunnel. This is extremely dangerous. Stay away from old tunnels that might be ready to cave in and watch out for open vertical shafts. Watch out for old chemicals and dynamite caps. Keep close track of children when in the vicinity of mines. Some mines are still active in the East Mojave. Give them a wide berth unless invited by the owners and operators. Respect any mining machinery you may see. It may not look in use but it may be a key element in some miner's operations. Historically, the mining industry opened much of the desert by providing a network of roads to support their operations. Many of these roads have become the "recreation trails" of today.

A campfire can be a welcome companion in a desert camp, but native wood is scarce. The rules permit you to collect "dead and down" wood for your own personal on-site use. You are not permitted to haul any wood off and you are not permitted to cut wood that hasn't fallen naturally. Be careful to watch where you place your hands while collecting "down and dead" wood -- you may accidentally expose yourself to some poisonous critter! Better still, plan ahead and bring your own supply of wood. If you burn trash, clean out the unburned material and take it home. Be sure your fire is extinguished before you leave. Don't destroy old buildings or artifacts to gain firewood.

TED JENSEN

It isn't uncommon for your camp to be visited by a
roadrunner. Remember the desert is their home and not
yours -- you are the visitor. Do not disturb them
unnecessarily. The kind of food supplies to bring on a
desert camping trip is a personal choice. Some people
eat from cans and spend no time at all on preparations,
leaving them free to enjoy the desert in other ways.
For others, preparing a full meal over a desert campfire
might be a vital part of the experience. Bring matches,
a can opener, tissues of all kinds, and plenty of water.
Be sure to bring adequate food and water supplies in
case of a breakdown in a remote spot.

Pop tents, like the one D. Ratt is dealing with in this
cartoon, are becoming increasingly popular with desert
campers. They take up little space in a 4WD and yet
they provide excellent protection from the elements and
can withstand the heavy desert winds. There's a great
variety of them with a corresponding variety in cost.
Some are much easier to erect than others. It is worth
your time to shop around and find one that isn't much
trouble to put up. Success on a desert camping trip
depends upon careful planning and preparation. Be
sure you've got all the right equipment and know how
to use it. Pick your camp site carefully -- never camp
in a wash in the desert because of the threat of flash
floods.

Clear air, lots of exercise, and meals around the campfire, provide restful nights. And the nights can be
beautiful on the desert. If the moon is out, it will at
times be so bright it casts a ghostly shadow. If there
is no moon, you'll see "shooting stars" and real stars in
an abundance that you haven't witnessed before. If it
is dark, let the campfire fade and watch the sky and
soon you'll pick a satellite moving against the background of stars. A star guide is fun to have.
Temperature extremes are experienced on the desert.
Most visitors expect it to be hot at least part of the
time, but many are surprised at how cold it can be
also, especially at night. It can be both "hot" and
"cold" during the same trip. Be sure to bring
necessary clothing to cope with both extremes.

It isn't likely you'll be attacked and bitten on the foot by a "Mojave Road Toad," like D. Ratt is in this cartoon. But bites and accidents do happen on the desert. Take a first-aid kit and know what's in it and how to use it. Know what you're going to do in case of a serious accident, like a broken bone or bite by a poisonous snake. Even simple accidents can become life threatening in the desert environment with difficult terrain and great distances to go for help.

TED JENSEN

Part of the great charm of the East Mojave is the pristine scenic beauty. For most visitors the presence of trash spoils all that. Carry your trash home. If the other guy has been more careless and left trash laying around, then carry his trash home too. The watchwords are: "If you haul it in, haul it out -- plus some" and "Always leave an area cleaner than you found it!" Also, don't leave a mess of trash at local businesses unless you ask.

.9   point to proceed). The point at which the Mojave Road
      leaves the Cedar Canyon Road is not well marked.
      We've put up cairns; but the Cable Road is immediately
      adjacent to the Cedar Canyon Road at this point so
      there is some confusion. As you leave the Cedar Can-
      yon Road, you drive on the Cable Road for about 0.1
      miles at which point the Mojave Road is a faint trace
      leading off to the right at a shallow angle. The old trail
      is indistinct as it heads west here because the presence
      of the Cedar Canyon Road has kept any appreciable
      traffic off it for many years. (0.5).

.4   A major road, the Death Valley Mine Road, crosses here
      going north and south (this road is not a maintained
      county road like the Cedar Canyon Road, but frequent-
      ly it is well traveled -- 4WD required at times). The
      track of the old Mojave Road is blocked by a fence line
      here. There is private land on the other side of the
      fence with no way through. It is necessary to turn left
      (south) on the Death Valley Mine Road, take it 0.2
      miles back to the Cedar Canyon Road, and then follow
      the Cedar Canyon Road to the intersection with the
      Kelso-Cima Road, where the original route of the old
      Mojave Road is rejoined at Mile 62.6. Of course, you
      are very close to the old trail throughout this detour.
           The Death Valley Mine Road is quite an historic
      route of travel in its own right. It served as one of the
      major thoroughfares in this country during the mining
      period at the turn of the century and thereafter pro-
      vided the connection between the mouth of Cedar
      Canyon and Cima. That road can still be used to reach
      Cima. It is slower than taking the Cedar Canyon and
      Kelso-Cima Roads to reach Cima, but it is much more
      picturesque, passing, as it does, through a beautiful
      Joshua tree forest and historic mining area. (3.2).

6   Intersection with Kelso-Cima Road. Approximately 2.4
      miles before reaching this point, the Cedar Canyon
      Road becomes blacktop. At Mile 62.6 you cross a cattle
      guard and the U.P.R.R. and immediately you are at the
      Kelso-Cima Road, where there are signs that say:
      "Cedar Canyon Road -- Hole-in-the-Wall Recreation Site
      17 miles, Mid Hills Campground 12 miles" (both being
      back up Cedar Canyon and Black Canyon Roads).
      Distances from this intersection to points of interest
      are: north on Kelso-Cima Road to Cima 4.4 miles, or to
      I-15 a total of 21.8 miles (there is a very small store
      and post office in Cima. Gasoline is not available in
      Cima. Gasoline and refreshments and some supplies are
      available at a service station at the Cima Road offramp

TEAMING IN THE EAST MOJAVE

Most wagons traveling the Mojave Road made use of mule and horse teams. This 14-horse team is headed from Death Valley Mine toward Cima, just a few miles north of the Mojave Road at Mile 59.4.

J. Riley Bembry Collection

.6   on I-15); the distance south on the Kelso-Cima Road to Kelso is 14.4 miles, or to I-40 via Kelso a total of 35.2 miles (there are no supplies available at Kelso nor at I-40 where this road reaches that highway). To continue on the Mojave Road, cross the Kelso-Cima Road and once again the Mojave Road becomes a primitive wagon road. The country ahead is primitive and isolated. You will not be near good high-speed roads again until you reach the Kelbaker Road at Mile 85.8. Do not attempt this stretch with only one vehicle. Be sure you have adequate supplies of gasoline and survival provisions. There is a fence line and cattle guard. This fence line is one of the main range fences for the Kessler Springs Ranch. The cattle guard was installed here on October 12, 1985, by the California Association of Four Wheel Drive Clubs as one of their improvement projects on the Mojave Road Recreation Trail. (0.3).

.9   Cross large Kelso Wash. For the next four miles there is considerable roughness in the road caused by cross-washing because the water from storms along this stretch flows at nearly right angles to the road. If you maintain low speeds, this is not bothersome. In fact, this stretch is one of the prettiest along the trail, partly because it has such a classic wagon road appearance, and partly because the views from here are so vast and beautiful. Of course, the presence of Joshua trees lends much to the charm. The observant traveler will notice that for the next several miles the road actually runs along the lower side of the southern slope of the Cima Dome. (1.6).

5   The names "Mojave Road" and "Old Government Road." Frequently someone asks the question "What is the difference between "Old Government Road" and "Mojave Road?" It turns out they are one and the same. And while you're bumping along this long open stretch and enjoying the beautiful vistas, and asking yourself why it is you'll have to return to "civilization" in a day or two, let us consider the matter of these two names.

We use the name "Mojave Road" because that's very nearly the name applied to this route of travel throughout the period that it served as an important transdesert trail. The name "Old Government Road" has been used for quite a long time by many people, but it is not historically accurate. It acquired a degree of respectability because the name has been used so much in modern times. It is interesting to consider how this misnomer has been placed upon the land. Perhaps this is how it happened.

115.

64.5   Today we have roads and highways with names and numbers. But in the old days, it was not that way. People often referred to roads in a more descriptive geographical fashion. Often the name told where the road went. Hence, we had the Oregon Trail and the Santa Fe Trail. During the period that the Mojave Road was important as a transdesert route, its purpose was to connect the seaport of Los Angeles with the capital of Arizona Territory. Then why wasn't it called the "Prescott Road" by contemporaries? Very simple. There were two roads to Prescott. The Mojave Road went through Cajon Pass and crossed the Colorado River at the site of the Mojave Indian Villages either at Fort Mojave or Hardyville. The other went through San Gorgonio Pass and crossed the river at La Paz or Ehrenberg, opposite the present Blythe. Calling either road the "Prescott Road" would have led to confusion. So people tended to call the northern road the "Mojave Road," "Hardyville Road," "Fort Mojave Road," or something like that. Probably "Fort Mojave Road" was used more than any other form. "Los Angeles to Fort Mojave Road" was not uncommon. The southern road was called the "La Paz Road," "Ehrenberg Road," or "Bradshaw Road" (William Bradshaw was one of the founders of the route).

          Another point to keep in mind is that the period of importance of this route as a transdesert trail was before the advent of the railroad between Barstow and Needles. After the coming of the railroad, the Mojave Road continued to be used to serve local needs, but it was no longer a road of more than local importance. Hence, the name should apply to the earlier period. Because this route of travel was originally a Mojave Indian trade trail, and the Mojave Indians had guided the first Americans that crossed the Eastern Mojave Desert over this route, we decided to shorten the name to "Mojave Road," so that it would refer to prehistoric as well as historic use.

          The question of where the name "Old Government Road" came from naturally arises. Interestingly enough, the only government road work to be done on the 35th Parallel Route in the 1850s went no farther west than the Colorado River. Edward Fitzgerald Beale's instructions were to take his camel caravans and construct a road from Fort Defiance, New Mexico Territory, to the Rio Colorado of the West. He went on west of the Colorado; but, he was not required to do that, and he did not mention this work in his official reports.

116.

It is true, however, that the Government made extensive use of this route of travel, as it did nearly every other major wagon road in the frontier west. During the 1860s it was the main route for military traffic for much of Arizona. It was also at one time the official route of the U.S. mail connecting California and Arizona. These uses may have given the route a "government road" flavor in the minds of some people.

The first permanent residents of the East Mojave, miners and ranchers, came to live there after the Mojave Road had already fallen out of use as a transdesert route. They had heard something of its history involving the military, the government camels, and other government use, so evidently they decided to call the route "Old Government Road." Some references to it by this name are nearly 80 years old.

One of the best maps of the East Mojave appears in "Route to Desert Watering Places in the Mohave Desert Region, California, Geological Survey Water Supply Paper 490-B," by David G. Thompson, published in 1921. Thompson refers to the trail as "Old Government Road to Fort Mohave." This was a mixture of historical truth and local tradition. When the U.S.G.S. later shortened the name, they dropped the wrong part. They dropped the part that was historically accurate.

The Mojave Trail became a wagon road in 1859. Until then it was merely a pack trail, although a few wagons had been taken over it. In July of 1859 the Los Angeles newspaper Southern Vineyard first faced the issue of a name by calling it "The Beale Route," or "The Road from Los Angeles to Fort Mojave." Thereafter, maps, the contemporary press, and military archives from 1859 to 1868 contain similar references to the road.

"Fort Mojave Road" would probably be the name that would best describe the road during the wagon road period (1859-1883). But, to encompass the pre-wagon road exploration period, and in deference to the Indians whose route it originally followed or evolved from, we call it simply "Mojave Road." (1.0).

In the literature of the California deserts, the word "Mojave" is spelled with both the "j" and the "h." This is another of those things where no particular approach is the correct one. The important thing is to pick a convention and stick with it. In this book the spelling "Mojave" is used for everything. The county by that name in Arizona is officially spelled "Mohave" so if any

65.5   reference to it was made, the "h" would be used, but otherwise the "j" is used except in direct quotations. In quotations the form chosen by the original writer is preserved.

Likewise, a convention is needed for the word Piute. In the old days they tended to use a hyphenated form like Pah-Ute. But simpler forms like Paiute and Piute have been used for many years. The form "Piute" is used in this book except in quoted material where the spelling of the original writer is preserved. (1.3).

66.8   This is a beautiful spot for a break. If you camped somewhere in Lanfair Valley or Round Valley the first night out, then you are ready for a morning break. You have a magnificent view of the Providence Mountains, Kelso Valley, the U.P.R.R. track with perhaps a train laboring along it, the Kelso Dunes, and much more. Traveling over this rough stretch has sometimes given rise to questions about how breakdowns by wagons in the old days were handled. What if a traveler was on a stretch like this and the wagon broke down? It turns out the people of those days were amazingly self-reliant and patient. It wasn't uncommon for wagons to break down. The wagonmasters carried basic blacksmith tools with them and had spare pieces of metal and seasoned oak wood strapped underneath. If need be, they would camp somewhere for a week working on their equipment if that was what was required to make the necessary repairs. Then they'd move on. And they'd go through that experience without feeling they had been struck by disaster. It was all in a day's drive! It should be noted that the road from the Colorado River to this point was considered to be an excellent wagon road, except, of course, the hill over Piute Mountain. The bumpiness did not bother slow moving wagons much. The important thing was that the grades were not bad and basically the soil was fairly firm. The most difficult stretches of road are ahead of you yet farther on to the west. Sand was the great impediment to efficient travel through the Soda Lake and Mojave River country. But to this point, heavy sand was not encountered. So, from the river to here was a very good wagon road. (0.5).

67.3   Intersect with improved road directly ahead and to the left. Road to the left goes to a mine in the Beale Mountains that has been worked in recent years. The existence of such mines illustrates another aspect of the multiple-use philosophy used to manage the public lands in the desert. On the same general acreage you may

118.

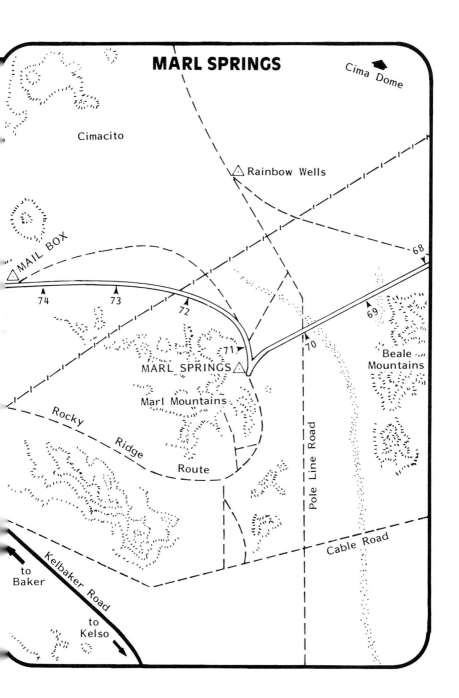

MARL SPRINGS

Cima Dome

Cimacito

△ Rainbow Wells

△ MAIL BOX

74 73 72

71 ▶

MARL SPRINGS △

Marl Mountains

68

69

70

Beale Mountains

Rocky

Ridge

Route

Pole Line Road

Cable Road

to Baker

Kelbaker Road

to Kelso

119.

67.3   simultaneously encounter cattle grazing, a mining operation, and people experiencing educational or recreational pursuits. Continue on the road directly ahead. (0.5).

67.8   At this point the Mojave Road bends southwest around the point of the mountains to the left leaving the improved road we have been on which continues northwest. Watch your mileage. Look for cairns so you don't miss this turn. If you find yourself still on a road bending toward the northwest, then you've probably passed the turnoff, and you'll have to go back. We have good cairns at the fork. The road that heads off to the northwest goes to Rainbow Wells, which is inhabited. (0.9).

68.7   Cross a large wash. You are at a point of the mountain here and will now be striking out across an open area toward Marl Springs. The Marl Mountains lie directly ahead at a distance of less than two miles. You still have a beautiful view of the Kelso Dunes off to the left for the next mile or more. WARNING: trappers are at work during the winter trapping season along much of the Mojave Road, and especially between here and Seventeenmile Point. They have many (over 100 at times) large steel traps set out for coyotes and bobcats. If you have a dog with you, he can be badly injured in one of these traps. It has happened to people traveling the road before. (0.8).

69.5   You are justified in keeping your eyes open for wild burros while driving into Marl Springs. In fact, the country from there to the lava flows and cinder cones area is a favorite haunt for these colorful and controversial animals. The burro problem out here has constituted a real management challenge in recent years. Twenty years ago there was no burro problem here at all. There were wild burros, but never enough to constitute a threat to anything. Their numbers were held at a reasonable level because cattle ranchers would thin them out if there got to be too many.

Then came the passing of the Wild Horse and Burro Act and problems for the BLM. Killing the burros was prohibited, so these prolific animals multiplied. The BLM tried capturing them for adoption but found that some of the adoptees were making a profit from the sale of burros to pet food manufacturers. To halt this, BLM had to follow up the adoptions with later inspection of the uses made of the burros. The problem still exists and the whole thing is very expensive to taxpayers. Perhaps the old way was better after all. The presence of a few burros on the East Mojave does not seriously

ADOBE AT MARL SPRINGS

Throughout the wagon road period there was a mixture of adobe, stone, and dugout buildings at Marl Springs. The adobe structure shown in this picture has disappeared. This picture was taken in 1931.

J. Riley Bembry Photo

MARL SPRINGS

A general view of the corrals and lower spring area at Marl Springs. The Marl Springs site is private land. It is an important watering place for the cattle grazed near there. The cattle are reluctant to approach the water troughs while you are there. Do not linger long by the water and never camp in the immediate vicinity. November 28, 1979.

Dennis Casebier Photo

122.

RUINS AT MARL SPRINGS

Marlou Casebier standing next to one of the stone ruins at Marl Springs. This structure is believed to have been one used by the U. S. Army at this site in 1867 and 1868. February 9, 1975.

Dennis Casebier Photo

69.5   interfere with cattle raising or with wildlife and they
        are desirable as a reminder of their ancestors and their
        masters who prospected far and wide over this area
        many years ago. (0.5).

70.0   Intersection with north-south pole line road. If you
        take this road to the south, it is 10.5 miles to the
        Kelso-Cima Road at a point 1.2 miles northeast of Kelso.
        (0.8).

70.8   Arrive at Marl Springs. There are two springs at Marl
        Springs, an upper spring and a lower spring. The
        lower spring is down near the corral. The Army fort
        and later way station were by the upper spring, about
        0.1 miles north of the lower one. The remaining
        arrastra is at the lower spring. It's usually more
        convenient to park by the lower spring, especially if
        you have a caravan of any size, because there's a big
        loop there for turning around. Please do not camp
        closer than 0.3 miles from the springs so as to allow
        unrestricted access by the cattle and wildlife.

        Creosote is the prevailing bush at Marl Springs.
        Joshua trees grow near there, but not right down to
        the springs. It may be they were used for fuel in the
        old days when large trains were coming through and
        camping here. Almost every train that came by camped
        at Marl Springs because it was over 30 miles westward
        to the next water. There's quite a variety of cactus
        growing in the vicinity including silver, buckhorn, and
        pencil cholla.

        It was Army Lieutenant Amiel Weeks Whipple who
        gave Marl Springs its name, on March 7, 1854, as
        Whipple was guiding his railroad surveying party along
        the 35th Parallel of North Latitude. Of course, the name
        was intended to be descriptive of the "marly" clay-like
        soil that surrounded the springs. Later the name be-
        came attached to the adjacent mountains.

        Because of its location, Marl Springs might be
        thought of as the most vital water source on the Mojave
        route. To the west the road begins to go downhill into
        the more barren and heated desert -- down into the
        fearful country of the Devil's Playground and into the
        Soda Lake and Mojave Floodplain country. It is more
        than 30 miles west from Marl Springs to Soda Springs,
        the nearest certain water source on the western edge of
        Soda Lake.

        It is difficult to say what distance between water
        holes would make a wagon road impractical in desert
        country. Of course it involves a combination of many
        things. But the complexities and rigors of the Mojave

Road were such that those 30-odd miles between Soda
Springs and Marl Springs were just about the limit. If
Marl Springs had been much smaller, or if it had been
of the intermittent type, then it might have put the
entire Mojave route into the "impractical at least part of
the year" category.

For a brief period (October 5, 1867 through May
22, 1868) an army post was maintained at Marl Springs.
It was called "the outpost at Marl Springs" by the
Army. In recent years, some writers have coined the
name "Camp Marl Springs," but it was never called that
by the Army.

Throughout most of its brief history, only a few
men were stationed regularly at "the outpost at Marl
Springs." These were men from Company "K" 14th
Infantry, which was stationed at Camp Rock Spring and
Camp Cady. On October 17, 1867, when the little stone
outpost building with the associated corral was being
completed at the upper spring, a band of desert Indians, estimated at 20 to 30, attacked the station. This is
probably the only occasion on which the desert Indians
attacked a fortified position along the Mojave Road in
California. There were only three soldiers there at the
time, and they took shelter in their partially completed
outpost building.

Night came on. The Indians were still holding
siege. They had a large numerical advantage, but the
soldiers had rifles and revolvers. All through the long
night the soldiers remained on guard expecting an
attack. They must have wondered what their fate would
be the next day. Would the Indians storm their fortified
position or would something happen to lift the siege?

In the best traditions of the romantic old West,
early the next morning a column of more than 150
soldiers came over the hill and down into Marl Springs.
The Indians melted into the rocks and disappeared. The
siege was lifted. There had been no casualties -- only
anxious moments. Marl Springs was never attacked
again.

There was never any major settlement at Marl
Springs, but during the wagon road period, it was not
uncommon to find someone living there. Citizens operated "stations" there at times, places where travelers
could purchase a few groceries, maybe a little grain,
perhaps a meal, or even a place to lay his head down
inside out of the elements for one night. These were
never elaborate establishments. There would be just a
man with his family and possibly a few Indians as

70.8   laborers.

After the wagon road period, Marl Springs continued as a station on the Mojave Road. As the cattle industry developed on the East Mojave, it became a place of importance for that purpose, and it still is. Headquarters for one of the earliest cattle operations on the East Mojave was at Marl Springs. Today there is a corral and watering facilities for cattle and wildlife, but no buildings.

Marl Springs has also served as an operations point for prospectors and miners in this part of the desert. Very near Marl Springs there are some small, but rich, gold-bearing veins in the rock that miners and prospectors worked over the years. Quite a number of arrastras were built at Marl Springs. One is well preserved yet today, though the others have disappeared. Local tradition has it that these arrastras go back to the very early days, the 1860s or 70s. There is no definite data to support this, but they were observed looking quite old in the early 1930s. A small ore mill was erected at Marl Springs, probably in the 1920s. Most of the timbers have been carried off, but the site is still visible.

Today Marl Springs is in an isolated far corner of the East Mojave, as it has always been. The immediate vicinity is private property, and it is used as a watering place for cattle. The land has never been posted. Our good behavior and sensitivity to the rights of the landowner and his cattle is the best assurance against its becoming posted. At times, a great many half-wild range cattle are totally dependent upon this water. It will always be advisable not to camp near the springs because there will be cattle too timid to come to water.

MOJAVE ROAD ON CIMACITO
The Mojave Road Recreation Trail on "Cimacito" looking
north toward the Cinder Cones and Lava Flow area
southeast of Baker, CA. December 27, 1982.
Dennis Casebier Photo

70.8   Leaving Marl Springs. It should be noted that the very earliest wagon road went south out of Marl Springs, whereas the route we've laid out goes north from that point. The southern route was abandoned very early (1859) because of a bad hill (Rocky Ridge) and much loose sand on that route. The northern route has no bad hills and less loose sand. As a main road and driving trail, we have marked out and will follow the road that leads north. The southern route can be used for hiking and exploring. It is called the ROCKY RIDGE ROUTE and it is discussed as a side trip at Mile 79.2.

 It is easy to get on the wrong road leaving Marl Springs to the north. There is also a heavily traveled road that goes north and east. Just above the upper spring the Mojave Road takes off as a faint trace more directly north and then even northwest, staying in close to the main line of the Marl Mountains. The correct route is well marked with cairns, but cattle use of this area is heavy and the cairns could get knocked down. The point where the Mojave Road takes off to the left of the more modern road is 0.15 miles above the loading chute of the corral at the lower spring. (0.5).

71.3   You have a choice of two roads here. They come back together at Mile 74.3. They are equally picturesque and represent roughly the same level of difficulty, so it is entirely up to the driver which way he wants to go. This narrative takes the road to the left. (0.9).

72.2   Pass under the Edison Company Power Line Road. (The power line service road will take you to the Kelbaker Road in 5.0 miles to the left [southeast]. It is a fair road.) To continue on the Mojave Road do not turn onto the power line road. Continue straight across under the power line. There is a good view of Cima Dome off to the right, and behind is a beautiful view of the Providence Mountains. (1.0).

73.2   This stretch is a wilderness area. Except for the power line there is little visible that represents the works of man. Also, until the Kelbaker Road is reached, there are no close paralleling roads that could mislead you. Of course, the area is blessed with beautiful vegetation and geological scenery, so all in all, it is one of the most beautiful stretches from a wilderness or natural point of view along the Mojave Road. At about this point, on either road, you come up over a summit and suddenly the magnificent lava flow and cinder cones area is spread out below and before you. You'll be

.2   going right by that area. The Cinder Cones will be the
      predominating feature until you turn the point of the
      mountain at Seventeenmile Point (Mile 88.0). Far be-
      yond, to the west of the Old Dad Mountains, you can
      see Soda Lake standing out as a white streak against
      the darker Springer Mountains. Beyond that, you can
      see Cave Mountain, at the left (southern) edge of which
      is Afton Canyon through which the Mojave Road passes
      on its way to Camp Cady. For a few minutes yet you
      can still see the Providence Mountains and Kelso Dunes
      behind you, and to the northwest there is a wonderful
      view of Cima Dome. In front of you there is as pretty a
      stretch of preserved wagon road to be found anywhere.
      This is a good place to stop, get out, and wave your
      arms and point. If your soul is susceptible to the
      beguiling effects of wilderness, then you will be enrap-
      tured at the feelings you can experience at this spot.
      Many others who have traveled the Mojave Road have
      sensed the great beauty and magic of this area. Dick
      Yet wrote that when he ran the trail in the spring of
      1981, in passing through this region, in imagination he
      could "hear the creaking of springs and the metallic
      sound of wagon wheels on rocks and the snorting of
      horses." Creosote bush is more sparse here. Pencil,
      buckhorn, and silver cholla are numerous. There are
      good representations of Spanish bayonet, Mohave yucca,
      and Joshua trees. Purple sage also grows here.
          You can get the feeling that you are sitting on top
      of the world. This is a majestic point -- majestic is the
      word. If you stop and think, you can visualize that
      nothing would have looked any different if you had
      been sitting here in a wagon in 1863. It's wilderness --
      and yet there is this nice 4WD trail running right
      through the middle of it. That trail, the Mojave Road,
      can be used to let the average person have a 4WD
      wilderness experience. It does not hurt the trail to
      drive it -- in fact, the trail will fade away if it isn't
      used. It will erode into ditches or disappear altogether
      through natural forces. (1.1).
3   Junction with the alternate branch of the Mojave Road
      (it comes in on the right). At this intersection, on the
      north side of the road, we have erected a metal mail
      box. There is a book in the box in which you can
      record the names of individuals in your party and the
      date of your passing and also your impressions of the
      Mojave Road Recreational Trail. The statistics and other
      information accumulated in the book over time will be
      used by the Friends of the Mojave Road and the Bureau

MAIL BOX ON THE MOJAVE ROAD
Spence Murray, Dick MacPherson, and Dennis Casebier at the Mail Box on the Mojave Road. There is a journal here and every traveler signs in. Mile 74.3. July 31, 1983.

Ralph Seegert Photo

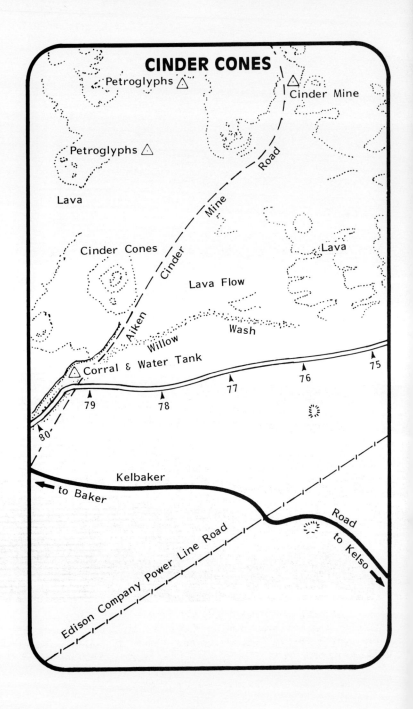

CINDER CONES

Petroglyphs △

Cinder Mine △

Petroglyphs △

Lava

Cinder Cones

Cinder Mine Road

Lava

Lava Flow

Aiken

Willow Wash

△ Corral & Water Tank

79   78   77   76   75

80

Kelbaker

← to Baker

Edison Company Power Line Road

Road to Kelso →

AERIAL RECONNAISSANCE ON MOJAVE ROAD
Chuck Thomas and Dennis Casebier fly over a caravan on the Mojave Road near Cimacito doing aerial photography and reconnaissance work. February 23, 1986.

Spence Murray Photo

133.

74.3   of Land Management as an input to management decisions effecting the trail. So, please watch for the mail box and stop and sign in! Give us the number of vehicles and people in your party as well as your narrative comments. (0.2).

74.5   Range fence with cattle guard. The cattle guard here, and the one at Mile 74.8, were installed in March of 1986 by a crew of volunteers under Mike Fascinato and Paul Winters, of the Victor Valley Four-Wheelers, and representing the southern district of the California Association of Four Wheel Drive Clubs. (0.3).

74.8   Range fence with cattle guard. This range fence and the one at Mile 74.5 mark the boundary between the Kessler Springs Ranch (behind you) and the Valley View Ranch (ahead of you). Just beyond this point the San Bernardino Mountains are visible in the distance. There are still scattered Joshua trees mixed with other desert vegetation. (2.2).

77.0   Road begins to get sandy. Sand will become worse in the next two miles, as the road continues to descend toward the lower desert. (0.1).

77.1   U.S.G.S. bench mark (elevation 3,535 feet) on left (south) of road. Still a few scattered Joshua trees, but they are thinning rapidly as the road descends. (0.2).

77.3   Sand gets worse. The driving can be difficult if the sand is dry and if there has been traffic ahead of you to churn up the loose sand. Recent rains tend to pack the sand and make it firmer until it dries out again.

You are traveling over the longest waterless stretch of the Mojave Road. It is more than 30 grueling miles from Marl Springs to Soda Springs. Detours caused by heavy mud in the lake could add five or even more miles. Difficulties were produced by the great difference in elevation (Marl Springs 3,800 feet and Soda Springs about 1,000 feet) and in the Soda Lake country there is heavy sand. The most heavily laden wagons were military and civilian freight wagons bound for Arizona Territory -- in other words, when loaded they were traveling from west to east, uphill, and through heavy sand, over a stretch that was more than 30 miles without water. That was actually more than could be done in a day.

Most of the segments between water holes on the Mojave Road -- for example, Colorado River to Piute Creek or Piute Creek to Rock Spring or Government Holes, or Rock Spring to Marl Springs -- were an easy day's drive. But the trek between Soda and Marl Springs could not be made in a day. When it was warm (which was much of the year), the teamsters would leave Soda Springs in the middle of the night. They would try to get to Seventeenmile Point by daybreak. They would rest their animals, feed them, give them water they had brought in kegs, and then try to push on to Marl Springs. Sometimes the teams would give out. It might be necessary to unhitch the teams, take the animals and water kegs on to Marl Springs, and after resting, return out here to retrieve the abandoned wagons.

You are also on the edge of the country that was rendered most dangerous by Indians. The Indians camped in the vicinity of the lava flows and frequented the road between here and Afton (then Cave) Canyon. As has been mentioned, the desert Indians were weak in numbers and weapons. But they would watch the wagon road for a straggler and then strike when they had one isolated. And this was the stretch where the wagons could get spread out. More than once, unfortunate teamsters lost their lives in this country because their teams were too weak to keep up with the rest, causing them to fall behind their trains and, hence, become tempting targets for the watchful Indians.

All kinds of traffic made use of the Mojave Road during its heyday. It was not principally an emigrant trail, but some emigrants used it. It carried an immense amount of military traffic between California and Arizona. At times, extremely large commands passed over the route. In May of 1873, for example, a civilian train bound from Los Angeles to Prescott, consisting of thirty twelve-mule teams with 200,000 pounds of freight, passed over the Mojave Road.

Off and on, depending upon which routes had the mail contracts, stages plied the Mojave Road between California and Arizona. At those times, relay stations were maintained at the springs. There was a steady flow of traffic of a great variety over the Mojave Road for more than 20 years (around 1860-1880). Toward the end of that period, another element was added to the traffic passing over the trail -- sheep and cattle. Droves of sheep and herds of cattle had been driven to Arizona before, largely, for immediate consumption. In the mid-1870s, when the Arizona Apaches were finally considered to be subdued and were concentrated on reservations, vast rangeland that could be used for sheep and cattle was suddenly opened. Much of the livestock that was introduced to the ranges of northern and central Arizona passed over the Mojave Road.

77.3   During 1875, for example, more than 30,000 sheep (and perhaps as many as 50,000) were crossed over the river into Arizona at Hardyville alone; others were crossed at Fort Mojave. The waterless stretch between Marl Springs and Soda Springs took a terrible toll on the livestock. One account states that the bodies of dead sheep along some stretches near here were so close together that a person could step from one to the other without touching the ground -- that is, if a person was of such a mind! In this area, the creosote bush begins to dominate once again, with its pal the burrobush. Also you occasionally see paperbag bush. (0.1).

77.4   Some observant travelers notice there are notches in the tops of some of the cinder cones that are very near now. These are the result of active prospecting. Developers take bulldozers to the top and dig down a way to investigate the quality of the cinders that make up the various hills. (1.8).

79.2   The route of the Mojave Road crosses the Aiken Cinder Mine Road at this point. This is a good road, generally kept scraped and maintained by the companies with quarries to the northeast. If you need to pick up time, you can do so here by turning left on the Aiken Cinder Mine Road and traveling 1.3 miles to the Kelbaker Road. Then turn right on the Kelbaker Road (which is blacktopped). Follow the Kelbaker Road for 11.6 miles to a point where a Cable Road access road takes you to the left into Seventeenmile Point. You avoid the sand and relatively slow driving of Willow Wash this way. It puts you back on the Mojave Road at Mile 88.0. On the other hand, Willow Wash provides an interesting drive with good views of the lava flows and cinder cones; so if you are not particularly pressed for time, you may want to stick with the Mojave Road which continues directly across the Aiken Cinder Mine Road. There is heavy sand ahead in Willow Wash.

     To the right at this point, there are water tanks and troughs and a small corral a hundred yards or so north of the point where Aiken Cinder Mine Road is crossed. The water that is sometimes present here is piped all the way from Deer Spring on Cima Dome. Some years ago the pipe line continued on down Willow Wash, around by Seventeenmile Point, and on to the eastern edge of Soda Lake. The line is no longer functioning beyond the present corral, but as you proceed toward Soda Lake you'll see remnants of it.

From this point it is relatively simple -- although
time consuming -- to take a side trip to Rocky Ridge.
You should allow two to three hours for this. It is well
worth it if you've got the time. To get there: turn left
(southwest) on the Aiken Cinder Mine Road. In 1.3
miles you come to the blacktopped Kelbaker Road (to
the right this road leads to Baker and to the left it
leads to Kelso). You continue on across the Kelbaker
Road on the extension of the Aiken Cinder Mine Road
that leads on to the southwest (there are rock cairns at
the intersections). In 1.7 miles beyond the Kelbaker
Road you'll come to a relatively good road along the
base of the hills that runs at right angles to the road
you've been on. Your road stops here. You turn to the
left and travel in a southeasterly direction along this
new road. In 1.3 miles you come to a junction -- you
are approaching the high lines but you're about 0.3
miles from them yet. At this junction turn right (southwest). This road takes you up to the backbone of this
spur of the Kelso Mountains. As you go up, you're
converging with the Edison Company high lines. Along
the way there are several relatively faint roads that
lead off to the left and serve as access roads to the
high line. Hopefully you won't get drawn off on them.
The distance from that last intersection to the top of
the ridge is 0.9 miles. After 0.7 miles you pass under
the high line but must continue onward and upward
another 0.2 miles to the flat parking space under the
towers. To the west of this parking place, the land
falls off sharply down into Jackass Canyon. The service
road for the high line continues on in that direction but
you'll be parking right here. Generally speaking, that
service road is passable with 4WD vehicles, but, of
course, the condition of such roads can change quickly
in the desert. It is a very steep road. To reach Rocky
Ridge from here you're in for a bit of a hike. You park
here in this enlarged flat area under the high line
towers and commence your hike along the main backbone
of the ridge to the southeast. You're following an old
Indian trail part of the way. There's a line of small
cairns to show the way. The distance up the ridge to
the point where the old wagon road crossed at right
angles is 1,612 feet. Also there is a large cairn at the
top of Rocky Ridge. You can see the stones have been
moved aside all down the ridge where the wagons used
to go. (About a third of the way to Rocky Ridge is a

ridge going down that has been negotiated by bulldozers, probably when the high line was constructed. Some people have been tricked into thinking this is Rocky Ridge.) For the information of those who might decide to hike down the ridge and have someone pick them up below, the distance down the ridge to the intersection with the high line service road has been measured by our volunteers as 4,160 feet.

ROCKY RIDGE HISTORY

Rocky Ridge must be, without a doubt, one of the most incredible hills ever crossed by wagons and teams. We consider it justified to include a brief statement about it here because of its unique character and also to draw attention to the existence of this important historic and prehistoric relic.

After discovering the hill in 1970, we told some friends of much desert experience where it was. They went out and inspected it. Their enthusiasm for the site and admiration for those who negotiated such a hill equalled ours. They raised one important point, however, that must be dealt with here. "The hardest part of the whole story is going to be getting people to believe that it was a wagon road."

For background, it is useful to look at the map of the stretch of the old road from Marl Springs to Soda Springs. This stretch has several unique features to keep in mind when reading early accounts through this area.

First, it was the longest journey on the Mojave Road without water. The distance was about 35 miles -- or a little less depending on which of several routes the traveler took.

Second, a direct line from Soda Springs to Marl Springs ran right straight through the Old Dad Mountain region. That forced the traveler to go around those mountains to the north (passing the point called Seventeenmile Point today) or around to the south passing the mountains by way of Jackass Canyon.

Third, there is a dramatic change in elevation between Soda Springs and Marl Springs. Soda Springs is a scant 930 feet, while at Marl Springs the traveler reaches 3,900 feet, a gain of nearly 3,000 feet. That means, going from west to east, it was over 30 miles uphill!

Fourth, there was the blow sand of the Devil's

ROCKY RIDGE
Darelyn Casebier and Wes Chambers stand at the top of
Rocky Ridge looking west toward Old Dad Mountain.
The wagons actually went down the ridge directly in
front of them. October 15, 1975.
Dennis Casebier Photo

Playground to contend with. It can be seen on any map of the East Mojave, if the traveler went to the south of Old Dad Mountain (on the Jackass Canyon route), he had to intersect this sand; whereas, if he went to the north, he missed most of it.

The first hint we found (many years ago) that there was probably more than one route between Marl Springs and Soda Springs was from Whipple's map. The scale of this map is such that the exact route cannot be traced. However, it can be seen that he shows his route going south from Marl Springs instead of north as the later road went.

This discovery prompted a careful examination of the various maps and journals and sure enough it was clear that originally the Mojave Road went south out of Marl Springs and passed south of Old Dad Mountain by way of Rocky Ridge and Jackass Canyon. It is clear that this route, with its terribly steep hill, was not used after the fall of 1859. By that time the easier route around the north side of Old Dad Mountain had been found and everyone went that way.

Following is one of the many accounts that describes this difficult route over Rocky Ridge. This was written by Maj. William Hoffman, 6th Infantry, describing his passage through this country in January of 1859. He is headed from west to east.

"Having a long march to make (from Soda Springs to Marl Springs), and to cross a range of mountains where the road would require some working, we made an early start."

"For a mile or so found the same bunch grass as at the camp. It is nine miles to the entrance of the Canyon (Jackass Canyon) which leads to the ridge, the sand being very loose, and in my opinion impassable for loaded wagons. The Canyon is three miles in length to the foot of the ridge, ascending all the way, over soft sand and gravel. The ridge is half a mile in the ascent, very rocky, over the backbone of a spur of the chain, and in places the rise is so abrupt that only light wagons could pass."

"At the foot of the mountain is a deep gully into which the wagons had to be let down on one side and assisted out on the other, by the command. The last twenty five yards, at the top, the rise is so steep, that our wagon, in addition to its eight mules, had to be assisted up by thirty men, and I doubt if any number of mules could take up a loaded wagon."

"It appears from the looks of the country, that a

better route might be found by passing to the left, but this would add several miles to the distance without water."

"From the crest of the mountain, which I have called Rocky Ridge, to camp is twelve and a half miles, over a firm road which travel would make good, but the country is entirely destitute of grass. This camp ground furnishes nothing but greasewood. Marl Spring is at the foot of a high hill which is one of a cluster; a hole has been dug in the ground, two feet across, five or six feet long, with an inclined bottom, and this forms the spring the water being two to three feet deep in the deepest part."

In the following years, both the northern and southern routes around Old Dad Mountain were used. But even when traveling the southern route, Rocky Ridge was not used. Instead, travelers stayed in Jackass Canyon until the ridge was cleared and then headed east for an approach to Marl Springs from the north. As already mentioned, the Rocky Ridge was not used at all after 1859 and the early trace leading south out of Marl Springs was used very little.

A number of interesting artifacts (historic and prehistoric) have been found on and around Rocky Ridge verifying what is clearly shown in the existing contemporary documentation -- i.e., men and animals actually pulled wagons over this terrible hill.

To continue on the Mojave Road you must now return to the intersection with the Mojave Road and the Aiken Cinder Mine Road retracing the same route that led you up to Rocky Ridge.

Beyond the intersection with the Aiken Cinder Mine Road the old wagon road dropped into Willow Wash and followed it -- as indicated on the maps -- all the way to Seventeenmile Point at Mile 88.0. This is quite a sandy wash and can be a problem even with 4WD vehicles. If there has been traffic recently, the sand will be churned up and loose. As you start down Willow Wash, to make sure you're headed in the right direction and not going astray, study the map and note that your route is bordered on the right (east) by the cinder cones and lava flows and on the left (west) by the Kelbaker Road. Think of the route as being a slot between those two features. As the map shows, do not cross Kelbaker Road until Mile 85.8. (2.0).

At this point the lava flow comes right against the

LAVA FLOW NEAR WILLOW WASH
Associated Blazers of California take a lunch break at the edge of the Lava Flow and Cinder Cones area. Mile 81.2. March 30, 1980.

Dennis Casebier Photo

142.

2   wash. There is a cliff here approximately 20 feet high. There are caves and holes in the lava that were formed as it cooled. The sandy surface of the wash runs right up against these cliffs. It is an excellent place for a break. It is not wise to camp here overnight or for an extended period because of the threat of flash floods. (0.3).

5   The following is a geological description of the cinder cones area by Volunteer Steven C. Semken.

"The cinder cones and lava flows visible north of the Mojave Road, between Seventeenmile Point and Cima Dome, are part of an extensive field comprising nearly thirty volcanoes, all centers of geologically-recent activity. This area, also known as the Cima Volcanic Field, is itself one of many similar sites located throughout the southwestern United States; Pisgah and Amboy Craters, in the southern Mojave Desert, are other examples. These scattered volcanic fields are all significantly younger than most geological features in the Southwest and are characterized by the eruption of alkali basalt, a black rock containing minerals rich in magnesium, iron, and calcium. The oldest volcanoes in the Cima Field, situated near Halloran Summit, are estimated to be roughly ten million years of age. The less-eroded appearance of cones and flows to the south-west, near Old Dad Mountain, suggests that eruptions here were even more recent. This has been confirmed by geological and laboratory study. The latest lava flow, which issued from a breached crater and abuts the Mojave Road approximately three miles southeast of Seventeenmile Point, has been dated by U.C.L.A. geochemists at less than one thousand years old. This is late enough for the Cima Volcanic Field to be considered potentially active; the possibility of further eruptions cannot be ruled out."

"The Cinder Cones are termed 'monogenetic' volcanoes, meaning that they were formed by single, brief, eruptions of considerable violence. During each eruption, thin, swiftly-moving lava flows spread laterally while volcanic debris shot upward and piled to form a cone. The debris is composed of solidified basalt lava in various forms, rounded or elongated bombs and jagged, blocky cinders (referred to as 'scoria' by geologists). Lava and debris are commonly laced with pores (vesicles) which betray the onetime presence of gases and fluids in the molten rock, or magma, when it emerged from the earth. The true colors of the erupted materials are deep grey to jet black, but quite

143.

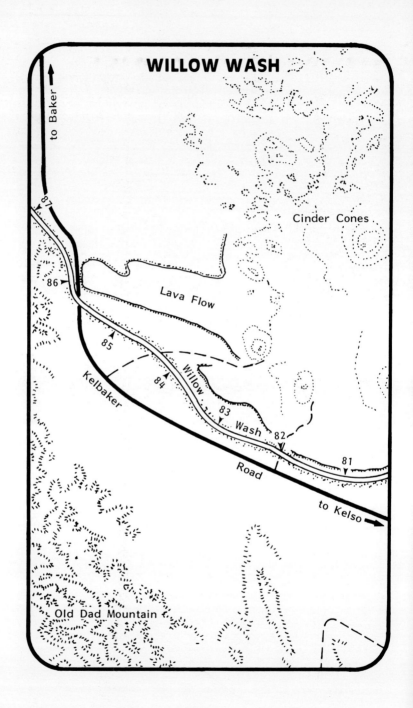

WILLOW WASH

to Baker

87

86

Cinder Cones

Lava Flow

85

84

Willow

83

Wash

82

81

Kelbaker

Road

to Kelso

Old Dad Mountain

144.

MOJAVE ROAD STEW

Bob and Marilyn Martin loading up with Mojave Road Stew in camp by Willow Wash on the Mojave Road. The evenings spent out on the trail, with associated meals and campfire "socials," are an important part of the Mojave Road experience. November 30, 1985.

Dennis Casebier Photo

CAMPFIRE

Much of the Mojave Road Recreation Trail is at higher elevations. It can be cold in the winter months. Here, Marlou Casebier and Craig Hodson warm the "other side" against the warmth of a blazing fire near Willow Wash. November 30, 1985.

Dennis Casebier Photo

5   frequently, iron-bearing minerals contained within have been oxidized during the concussive eruptions and color the rock brick-red."

"The Cima cones and other continental alkali-basalt volcanoes have erupted far smaller volumes of lava and debris than other types, such as the massive Cascade volcanoes. However, their interest to geologists is far out of proportion to their importance in forming continental crust. Alkali basalt is a close chemical relative of the materials believed to form the Earth's mantle, and alkali-basalt eruptions are unusual in that they carry 'xenoliths,' fragments of the surrounding mantle and crust torn away by the ascending magma and brought to the surface. These volcanoes are among the best 'windows' available to earth scientists seeking to understand processes which occur deep beneath the continents. The cinder cones and their like are also quite similar to kimberlite pipes, extinct volcanic conduits emanating from deep in the mantle, which are the sole source of natural diamond. However, their commercial importance is limited to quarrying cinders for use as building material and railroad ballast. Young volcanoes such as these are presently being investigated as indicators of potential sources of geothermal energy." (0.5).

Fairly good road crosses. This leads from Kelbaker Road on the left (0.2 miles) and up into the lava flow and cinder cone area on the right. If you're not in a hurry, a jaunt to the right a mile or two makes an interesting side trip. It is not considered safe to attempt to drive to the top of any of the cinder cones; also, it would constitute a negative environmental impact. The sides are loose cinders in many places. You'll notice what appears to be roads cut into the sides and going to the top of most of the cinder cones. These have been made and used by bulldozers operated by people prospecting for commercial grade cinders. If you have the time and energy, then, by all means, hike to the top of one of the cinder cones. You'll be treated to beautiful views of the lava flows, cinder cones, and surrounding country in every direction.

Continue across this road and down the wash. The sand in the wash can be quite loose, depending upon dryness and the amounts of recent traffic. As you come down this wash, the Avawatz Mountains stand out massively ahead in the far distance. The highway from Baker to Death Valley runs just to the right of those mountains. (1.1).

147.

STUCK IN THE SAND
When the sand is dry, Willow Wash can be treacherous. This picture shows a skillful driver (Jim Brokaw) with a 4WD stuck in the wash at about Mile 85.4 October 24, 1982.

Jim Crow Photo

NEAR SEVENTEENMILE POINT
The Jeep is in Willow Wash at about Mile 86.2 nearing
Seventeenmile Point. December 28, 1981.
Paul Lord Photo

83.1 The alkali-basalt lava flow on the right is the most recent one in the Cima Volcanic Field. The breached cinder cone from which it issues is visible to the east. (1.2).

84.3 Cross another road that goes into the cinder cone and lava flow area. There is a nice camping area a short distance up this road to the right. (1.0).

85.3+ You are now approaching the Kelbaker Road. Willow Wash will intersect it in about 0.5 miles. Every time water runs in Willow Wash the county has to come out and scrape the sand off of Kelbaker Road. When there are heavy floods the entire road may be washed out. This frequently results in considerable road grader activity at the point where the Mojave Road crosses Kelbaker Road, which means the sand can be churned up and, consequently, be extremely soft. If you're concerned about this -- and especially if you're traveling alone so there would be no one to pull you out -- you might want to take a more direct route to Kelbaker Road (off to your left). We have had 4WDs operated by experienced drivers get stuck in this loose sand! (0.5).

85.8 Cross Kelbaker Road. Willow Wash crosses the surface of the Kelbaker Road. There are no drainage pipes nor any bridge. A right turn on Kelbaker Road will take you to Baker in about 15 miles (for a discussion of services available in Baker see Mile 95.9). A left turn on Kelbaker Road will take you to Kelso in about 20 miles. To follow the Mojave Road, go directly across the blacktop and continue down Willow Wash.

At this point and a little beyond, the lava flows on the right and the Old Dad Mountains on the left form a stony gateway through which Willow Wash passes. (1.4).

87.2 Barrel cactus on the hills to the left and a few down on the flats. Avawatz Mountains loom large in the distance ahead and traffic on I-15 near Baker becomes visible. (0.8).

88.0 You are at Seventeenmile Point, so named because it was thought in the old days to be about 17 miles west to Soda Springs and 17 miles east to Marl Springs. This is the midpoint on the longest stretch on the Mojave Road without water. As you can see, it represents a point where the edge of the mountain mass meets the alluvium of the desert floor. Frequently in desert country the old routes of travel headed for these points which were often referred to as "point of the mountain." Thus, Seventeenmile Point got its name. The Mojave Road curves around the tip of the mountains at

SEVENTEENMILE POINT

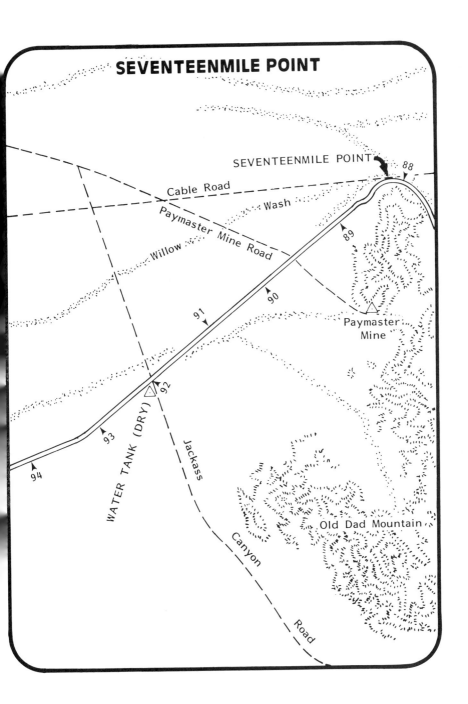

SEVENTEENMILE POINT

88

Cable Road

Wash

Paymaster Mine Road

Willow

89

90

91

92

WATER TANK (DRY)

93

94

Paymaster Mine

Jackass

Canyon

Old Dad Mountain

Road

151.

SOUTHWEST OF SEVENTEENMILE POINT
The Mojave Road (about Mile 88.0) looking southwest of Seventeenmile Point toward Soda Lake. December 27, 1982.

Dennis Casebier Photo

.0   Seventeenmile Point and heads on southeast. The underground telephone cable and the service road associated with it also passes around Seventeenmile Point.
But it heads more directly straight west. Do not get
pulled off on the Cable Road. The proper route is not
straight. If you find yourself traveling on a straight
road that heads directly toward Soda Lake after you
pass Seventeenmile Point, you can be assured you've
missed the turn. Go back to Seventeenmile Point and
try again! (0.0+).

.0+   As you curve around the mountain and head southwest,
there is a wonderful view westward across Soda Lake
and on toward Cave Mountain. Soda Lake can look quite
different at different times. As with so many things on
the desert, its appearance depends to a large extent on
how long it has been since the last rain. If it appears
as a bright white streak, then it has rained fairly
recently. Moisture on the lake brings salts to the
surface. The water evaporates, leaving bright white
chemicals. In time, dust blows in from the west and the
bright white appearance begins to fade. Soda Lake is
approximately 5 miles wide at the widest place, and
about 20 miles in length north and south. Baker and
I-15 are in full view from Seventeenmile Point and
beyond as you descend toward Soda Lake. You will
notice also that the more lush vegetation of the higher
elevations has given way to scattered creosote and
burrobush and very little else to break the scenery.
(1.5).

5   To the left of the road, there is a small patch of cinders and other remains that suggest something existed
here at one time. It was the site of a water tank on the
pipe line that runs buried under this road toward Soda
Lake. (0.1).

      Intersection with the Paymaster Mine Road. To the left
(southeast) a little more than a mile there is quite an
extensive mining area which is one of the oldest in this
part of the desert. In the old days, activity there
revolved around the extensive Paymaster Mine. To the
right in a distance of two miles you'll come to the Cable
Road. Continuing on the Paymaster Mine Road will take
you on to the Kelbaker Road and Baker. It is 8.8 miles
to Kelbaker Road from this point and another 1.2 miles
on to Baker. Paymaster Mine Road is quite a good one,
as is the Mojave Road in this area. Good time can be
made between here and the Cowhole Mountains on the
Mojave Road but there are some incidents of unexpected
roughness. (1.6).

91.2   Another water tank site, but, as with the one at Mile 89.5, there are no remains of the water tank. You can see where it was. Going down this road you'll notice that at times there are large numbers of rodent holes. There appear to be whole colonies of the creatures. If you get out and walk among them, you'll find yourself actually stepping into the shallow underground tunnels. They appear on both sides of the road and in places they have actually undermined and disrupted the surface of the road itself. (0.8).

92.0   Intersection with the Jackass Canyon Road. Continue straight. The road to the left becomes quite sandy and after the blow sand area is passed, it becomes quite rough and rocky. In about nine miles this road will bring you to the mouth of Jackass Canyon, just south of Old Dad Mountain, and the Edison Company Power Line. A left turn into Jackass Canyon will take you back to Kelbaker Road in about 10 miles. This provides an interesting and beautiful way to go around the Old Dad Mountain mass, but it is a long and difficult drive.

To the right the Jackass Canyon Road will take you back to the Cable Road in 2.5 miles and then in another 0.6 miles Jackass Canyon Road intersects the Paymaster Mine Road and hence you could travel on to the Kelbaker Road or Baker. However, Jackass Canyon Road is not as well-maintained or heavily traveled as the Paymaster Mine Road. It has more sand. There is a dry water trough at this intersection. This was another point served by the long pipe line that ran all the way from Cima Dome. Continue straight. (0.5).

92.5   As you drive along here, you're on the northern edge of a large area of blowing and drifting sand, the Devil's Playground. The eastern extension of that is the Kelso Dunes. This wonderland of sand is created by dust and sand being blown eastward out of the Mojave River Valley. The winds in this area almost always blow from west to east. There is a never-ending supply of lightweight soil. So it is constantly being blown in here. As it reaches this area, the land to the east begins to rise as the Providence Mountains are approached. The wind falls off in intensity, and the combination of rising land and decreasing wind velocity cause the sand and dirt to be deposited. This country can be extremely dangerous even with 4WD vehicles, and only the adventurous, intrepid, and experienced should venture in that direction. The Kelso Dunes themselves are "closed" by BLM, so no driving is permitted there under any circumstances. (1.2).

154.

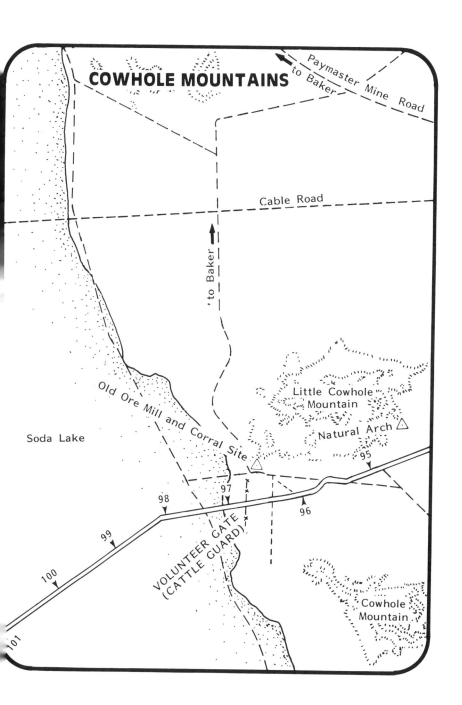

COWHOLE MOUNTAINS

Paymaster Mine Road

to Baker

Cable Road

to Baker

Old Ore Mill and Corral Site

Soda Lake

Little Cowhole Mountain

Natural Arch

95

97

96

98

99

VOLUNTEER GATE (CATTLE GUARD)

100

101

Cowhole Mountain

155.

NEARING SODA LAKE
The Mojave Road at Mile 96.6 looking west. The lighter-colored horizontal strip is Soda Lake. The mountain on the horizon is Springer Mountain. February 12, 1975.

Dennis Casebier Photo

3.7   Road bends slightly to the right, more directly toward Soda Lake. The way is marked with cairns. There are a number of side roads in the next few miles where you could possibly take a wrong turn. We've put up cairns at all of them, so if you'll watch closely for them, there shouldn't be any problem, but the road you're on right now is relatively fast (for a back country road) so you might miss a turn. (1.3).

5.0   Between here and Soda Lake there is an abundance of volcanic rocks of various sizes. Please stop for a moment and have everyone pick up one rock. This is to be added to a traveler's marker at Mile 101.1 called GOVERNMENT MONUMENT. Be sure to pick up a rock now, there won't be another chance once you're out on the lake. (0.1).

5.1   Road on left. Continue straight. (0.7)

5.8   Graded road comes in on left. It leads to the central part of the Cowhole Mountains where extensive prospecting has taken place. (0.1).

5.9   The Mojave Road turns to the left off the well-traveled road at this point. The best traveled route continues west and leads to the old mill site and corral at the southwestern corner of Little Cowhole Mountains. If you wind up at the corral and mill site, then you've gone too far and you'll have to backtrack. From here to Volunteer Gate, the road is quite rocky.

    If you wish, you can leave the Mojave Road to visit Baker from this point. Go to the mill site and turn north at that point and follow the road north to Baker. It will take you by way of the Baker Dump. Distance to Baker is about 8.5 miles from the Mill Site along the eastern edge of Soda Lake and along the western edge of Little Cowhole Mountains.

    Baker, Barstow, and Needles are the three main towns that serve travelers on the Mojave Road. Baker has a full line of services and is centrally located to the trail. Many will want to go there to spend a night, obtain provisions, gasoline, or enjoy some of the other amenities of civilization. Lois Clark of Baker has provided the following statement of the services available in her town.

    "Baker. Hub of the Desert. Many years ago Bob Hovely and Dad Fairbanks with foresight realized the need of a station to serve the traveling public. Dad first erected a tent with a porch; Bob erected a crude shack. The T & T Railroad made three stops a week: Highway 91 was a winding dirt road. That dirt road, as I-15, has now become the most direct route between Los

157.

95.9   Angeles and Las Vegas. It is a major freeway and the town of Baker is located at its junction with the main highway into Death Valley and with the road to Kelso providing access to the East Mojave National Scenic Area and connections with I-40 to the south."

"The town is ideal as headquarters for the sight-seer planning trips into Death Valley, Scotty's Castle, Hoover Dam, Las Vegas, Lake Mohave, Calico Ghost Town, Pahrump Valley, Tecopa Hot Springs, Dumont Dunes, Zzyzx Springs, or the East Mojave National Scenic Area."

"The colorful desert and surrounding hills with their vast treasure trove of vividly-hued rock and gem stones lure the "rockhounds" as well as the artist. An elevation of 970 feet above sea level provides Baker with mild pleasant winters -- attested to by the once-successful health resort at Fort Soda or Zzyzx, nine miles to the south."

"Four modern motels, three drive-ins, three garages (one AAA), two trailer parks, two mini-marts, one well-stocked general merchandise store, and service stations of most major gas companies supply the needs of the traveler and the town's 600 population. Baker also has a well-staffed ambulance service and volunteer fire department."

"Baker, named after Lord Baker, an English official of the T&T Railroad, has its own school district, including kindergarten through 12th grade, a Catholic Church, a non-denominational Christian Church, and a Mormon Church."

"Make Baker, where Death Valley meets the Great Mojave Desert, your rest stop or your sight-seeing headquarters." (0.1).

96.0   There's a "Y" in the road. Stay left. (0.4).

96.4   Intersection with north-south road. To the right this road will take you back to the good road you left at Mile 95.9 and hence on to the old mill site. To follow the Mojave Road continue directly across (west) this road toward the lake. (0.3).

96.7   The road reaches a range fence here, designed to keep cattle from wandering out on Soda Lake. The cattle guard here is called "Volunteer Gate" in honor of the FRIENDS OF THE MOJAVE ROAD and members of the RIVERSIDE RUFF RIDERS who constructed the gate and later installed the cattle guard. Nearing Soda Lake creosote and burrobush thin out and salt bush takes over. (0.4).

.1 As you leave Volunteer Gate, you enter the edge of Soda Lake, sometimes erroneously called Soda "dry" Lake. It is quite soft for the first tenth of a mile or so, because of the accumulation of dust and sand blown westward across the lake. But shortly you come to a hard surface where all loose material has been blown away. Beginning at Volunteer Gate and continuing out onto the lake, there are green metal fence posts driven into the ground to show the way. Near the shores of the lake these are placed at one-tenth mile intervals. Out on the lake, where there is less chance to make a wrong turn, they are spaced at intervals of two-tenths of a mile. (0.3).

.4 You are now on the edge of the softer parts of Soda Lake. Soda Lake is closed to off-highway vehicle use except for designated routes (including the Mojave Road). Do not drive on the lake or attempt to cross it on any other route. Even this route is impassable at times. This can be one of the most dangerous decision points on the Mojave Road. You must make at least a tentative decision about whether or not to attempt to cross the lake. It should never be attempted with one vehicle traveling alone. Considerable separation should be left between vehicles in case the lead driver gets stuck. Then you should have the means to extricate a vehicle that does get stuck. LOCK YOUR HUBS AND PUT YOUR TRANSMISSION IN 4WD NOW IF THEY ARE NOT ALREADY THERE. EVEN IF THE SURFACE LOOKS VERY DRY, YOU MAY NEED THESE EXTRA ADVAN-TAGES TO GET THROUGH AN UNEXPECTED STRETCH OF MUD! If you get to this point and decide you can't cross the lake, then you'll probably have to detour to the north to Baker. From Baker you can take I-15 to the Rasor offramp and then go down Rasor Road to intersect the Mojave Road at Mile 104.5. But there is another alternative. Sometimes you can pass to the south of Soda Lake when the lake cannot be negotiated directly. This is dangerous. The way is unmarked. No effort is made here to provide an accurate or recom-mended itinerary. There is sand and brush. There can be mud. But if you're an experienced four-wheeler looking for adventure, and have several vehicles in your group, you might want to try it. For the purposes of this Guide we will assume you are able to cross the lake or that you'll detour through Baker. (0.7).

.1 At this point in the old days, the Mojave Road contin-ued on straight across the lake to Soda Springs, now frequently called Zzyzx Mineral Springs or simply

CROSSING SODA LAKE
A group of vehicles from the California Association of Four Wheel Drive Clubs crossing Soda Lake. Foreshortening by the telephoto lense makes them appear "line abreast" whereas in fact they are single file. This picture was taken from the Granites looking east across the lake. October 24, 1982.

Paul Lord Photo

.1 Zzyzx. (Even in wagon road days, travelers sometimes had to deflect to the north or south -- usually north -- to avoid mud in Soda Lake.) You cannot go directly across the lake now because Zzyzx is a restricted area (see discussion of this and the history of Zzyzx at Mile 101.1). Consequently we have laid out the route to angle southward and bypass the restricted area. Where the turn occurs three metal fence posts have been placed in the middle of the direct line heading toward Zzyzx. This is designed to let you know you're at the point where you must deflect slightly southward. If you'll look in that direction, you'll see the metal fence posts continuing on across the lake. Do not proceed across the lake if you don't see the route you're sup- posed to follow. It can get confusing out there. If you lose the line of fence posts, go back to the eastern shore and try again. At times Soda Lake can be too muddy to cross under any circumstances. If you are in doubt about the condition of the lake, or in doubt about your ability to make a safe judgement, check with BLM before beginning the trek. (0.2).

.3 CAUTION!!! Here is the first (and very unexpected) of a few hidden, narrow, deep channels that lie in wait to stop your wheels while allowing the remainder of your vehicle to proceed. Despite the fact that Soda Lake looks flat and smooth from a distance, there are quite a number of usually dry watercourses that wind north- ward aiong the lake. The presence of these water courses discourages fast driving out on the lake. You can come up on them suddenly, and they can be quite deep. If you have doubts at all about whether the lake might contain some mud, be sure to stop at the edge of these watercourses and check them out on foot before crossing. Remember, Soda Lake is not open to unrestricted vehicle use. You must remain on the marked trail. This is not a free-play area. Stay on the road no matter how tempting the surface of the lake looks for frolicking. Leave it with an undisturbed appearance for the enjoyment of all. (1.5).

.8 Intersect the main water course. This one is quite deep and about 100 feet wide. It can contain a muddy bottom long after the others have dried out. Be sure to check it before entering with a vehicle.

All warnings and precautions aside, there will be instances where travelers on the Mojave Road will attempt the crossing of Soda Lake when it's too muddy. And if that happens to you, don't feel it's that you didn't pay attention. It's tricky and sometimes

SODA LAKE
At times the mud in Soda Lake can be so terrible it would be impossible for any wheeled vehicle to cross. At other times, as in this picture, it will be bone dry and you'll have to keep moving to keep ahead of the choking clouds of dust.

Paul Lord Photo

.8   unpredictable business. Soda Lake can fool you. And
       then of course some of us are just more adventuresome
       than others so we'll try it when it might be more pru-
       dent (conservative?) to do otherwise. There is no way
       all the difficulties can be anticipated and advice given
       about what to do in advance. Mike Dougherty, former
       caretaker at Zzyzx, has done some thinking on the
       subject and wrote the following ideas about surviving
       on Soda Lake:
            "I might suggest inclusion in the Guide special
       Soda Lake survival instructions. Suggested ideas: Don't
       travel alone. Use at least two rigs. Do not walk towards
       Baker. Walk towards the closest shore and then towards
       Baker. The shore will provide easier walking and
       shade. Have only the strongest person walk for help.
       Don't start walking until the sun touches the mountain.
       Zzyzx will provide emergency help for people, not
       vehicles. Carry a flashlight. Have and know how to use
       a handyman jack. Do not tire yourself out trying to get
       unstuck and then walk for help. Conserve your energy.
       Think about saving people first. Don't depend on CB.
       From the Mojave Road, Baker is at least four hours
       away if you are walking on firm ground. Know how to
       signal an SOS with headlights; fire doesn't signal for
       help, it only looks like another campfire. Stomp out an
       SOS in the mud for aircraft. Realize you have a serious
       problem."
            And at other times there will be no mud on Soda
       Lake, only heat. In some places there'll be great clouds
       of choking alkaline and salt laden dust. There will be
       places where there are long stretches of smooth black
       hard-packed surface soils that bake you from beneath
       while the sun bakes you from above. You can die on
       Soda Lake in the summer with water in your canteen. It
       is probably potentially the most dangerous stretch of
       the Mojave Road -- with the possible exceptions of the
       Floodplain of the Mojave between Shaw Pass and Afton
       Canyon or the sandy bed of the Mojave River above
       Afton Canyon. Proceed with caution. If you're alone
       and don't know what you're doing, don't proceed at all
       or you may well become a statistic!
            If the main marked route across Soda Lake is too
       muddy, turn around (or back out or however you can)
       and take the northern route through Baker. (0.3).
.1   An unexpected dropoff. Proceed slowly. (0.4).
.5   If any part of the lake is going to be muddy, this is
       the most likely. Almost always it will be a little sticky.
       The secret of success is to stay away from the shore

TRAVELERS MONUMENT
At Mile 101.1 on Soda Lake (at the point of closest approach to Zzyzx) each traveler on the Mojave Road pauses to add his rock to the growing pile known as "Travelers" or "Government" Monument. There is a special bronze plaque on this monument, but you must go there to learn what it says. These vehicles are headed from west to east whereas most travelers will be going from east to west. June 9, 1985.
Dennis Casebier Photo

0.5   until you get clear down by the Granites. Do not yield
      to the temptation to go ashore in the vicinity of Zzyzx,
      or you'll get stuck for sure. Stay on the road marked
      by the green posts. Stay in 4WD until you reach the
      Granites. If it looks like it might get muddy ahead of
      you, shift to low range and keep your speed up. If
      traffic has been heavy and conditions are marginal,
      then the beaten path becomes muddy because the weight
      of the vehicle forces water to the surface. Soda Lake
      mud is corrosive. Be careful in exposing vehicles and
      pets to it. Wash it off the vehicle after a trip. (0.6).

1.1   Traveler's or Government Monument. As you approach
      the western shore of Soda Lake, continue to angle
      southwest to avoid the restricted area at Soda Springs
      or Zzyzx. At this point you'll be about as close as
      you're going to get to Zzyzx unless special arrange-
      ments have been made. You'll want to stop here for a
      moment to add your rocks to Traveler's or Government
      Monument. If it is too soft to stop, just toss your rock
      near the monument and some future traveler will pile it
      up on a day when the surface is firmer. Note the brass
      plaque on the monument. Knowledge of the words on
      the plaque are restricted to people like you who have
      been there. Keep the secret!

101.1   If it isn't too hot or muddy, it would be a good time to take a break here at the monument and read about Soda Springs and Zzyzx and about the things that have gone on at that fascinating place in recent years.

Soda Lake received its name from Lt. Amiel Weeks Whipple as he brought his large surveying party through this country in March of 1854. His transit across the lake was a little to the south of the track we're following. He gave the name "Soda" to the lake due to its white appearance. He did not see Soda Springs, which later took their name from the lake. Probably the earliest reference to "Soda Springs" occurred in 1859. By that time the Mojave Road passed that way and Soda Springs had become a vital link in the chain of springs the road utilized crossing the East Mojave.

In 1860 a small army outpost was established at Soda Springs during the war with the desert Indians. It was called "Hancock's Redoubt" in honor of Winfield Scott Hancock, who at that time was Army Quartermaster in Los Angeles. This post was occupied by men of Companies "B" and "K" of the 1st Dragoons for just a short time. They build a fort-like structure of adobe, sticks, and rocks, that remained for several years.

During the 1860s Soda Springs continued to be a major stopping place on the Mojave Road. In 1867 the army established another post there. As with the other little outposts on the Mojave Road, it was maintained to provide escorts to the stages and U. S. mail. The outpost at Soda Springs, frequently referred to as "Soda Station," was subordinate to Camp Cady. It was not an official army post in its own right. It was never called a fort or camp by the army, but today many writers refer to the site as "Fort Soda" because of this historical connection with the army.

In early historic times there were several free-flowing springs at Soda, at least one of which was of impressive proportions. The water table has lowered over the years so that today, although there is an abundance of water just below the surface, there are no free-flowing springs.

After the wagon road period, about the early 1880s, Soda Springs was involved in a number of promotions connected with desert mining. At one time it had something of a population, probably mostly promoters, and was known as "Shenandoah Camp."

In 1906-1907 the Tonopah & Tidewater Railroad was built through this region and there was a siding at

01.1 Soda Springs. Encouraged by the availability of rail transportation, other developers constructed evaporating vats and other works to process minerals from the brine of the lake. Quantities of sulphate, salt, and sodium carbonate were produced. There was a small narrow-gauge track for ore cars extending a mile and a half out onto the lake to support the operation. The works were extensive and remains of them are visible today.

There are stories about a religious colony being developed here before 1920 by Russelites. But no definite data has surfaced.

It appears things were pretty lonely at Soda Springs in the 1920s and 1930s. The T&T trains continued to pass through at regular intervals, but they rarely stopped. It was a far corner of the desert, and only the most intrepid of desert explorers ventured there. There is an interesting account by mystery writer Erle Stanley Gardner of a visit he made there in 1938 to hunt frogs in the marshy ground that surrounded the springs.

In 1940 the T&T was abandoned and during World War II the rails were taken up. Soda Springs was abandoned and more isolated than ever before.

On September 13, 1944, Soda Springs history took a new turn. On that day its destiny became entwined with that of a controversial personality of great intellect, charisma, and magnanimity. On that day Soda Springs became ZZYZX -- and Dr. Curtis Howe Springer became, and will forever remain, the leading figure in Soda Springs history.

Soda Springs, with its extreme isolation, seemed ideal as a place to develop a resort. It had an endless amount of mineral water (some say it is capable of producing more than a million gallons per day) and it was on public land. The status of the site was checked with the land office. There were no claims against it. Dr. Springer and his associates were informed that they could place mineral claims on the land and commence development. This they did. They staked out approximately 12,800 acres of seemingly worthless desert land and their claims were duly recorded in the records of San Bernardino County.

At first they lived in tents with no electricity or refrigeration. An old pool was cleared out. Dr. Springer continued a series of radio broadcasts that he had pursued for many years that explained a line of health foods, and he began to mention his new resort,

ZZYZX MINERAL SPRINGS

When Zzyzx Mineral Springs was open to the public, signs like this were maintained on I-15 (and U. S. 466 before that) showing people the way and inviting them in. The remains of the signs are now in the Zzyzx dump. The Friends of the Mojave Road spent an entire day removing them from the dump and erecting them on an adjacent open spot for photographic purposes. December 31, 1981.

Dennis Casebier Photo

DR. CURTIS HOWE SPRINGER

Dr. Springer was the visionary and driving force behind construction and operation of Zzyzx Mineral Springs. This photo was taken on what was probably his most recent visit to Zzyzx in 1976.

Jerry Gates Collection

ZZYZX

Jerry Gates (now deceased) posed with a sign that
stood for many years on the Boulevard of Dreams at
Zzyzx welcoming visitors. It fell down a few years ago,
but has been restored and is now on display in one of
the buildings. July 21, 1980.

George Bieber Photo

ZZYZX FROM THE AIR
February 23, 1986
Dennis Casebier Photo

EXCAVATIONS AT SODA SPRINGS
Connie Cameron, of Cal State Fullerton, supervises an investigative archeological excavation at Soda Springs. The grave of a young Indian woman was found near here. April 17, 1980.
Dennis Casebier Photo

ZZYZX & LAKE TUENDAE
This shot shows Lake Tuendae and some of the buildings at Zzyzx Mineral Springs. The lake and the buildings were all constructed by Dr. Curtis Howe Springer and his wife Helen Springer over a period of nearly 30 years. December 1981.

Spence Murray Photo

101.1   Zzyzx Mineral Springs.

Zzyzx isn't an Indian name, as many suppose. It was created by Springer to be the last word in the English language. And, to date, it seems to hold that status without serious competition.

Over the next ten years the tents were replaced by buildings. A modern pool was built "in the shape of the Cross of Christ" with associated compartmented baths, which permitted guests to take mineral baths with water at a variety of temperatures. Provisions were made for mud baths. Accommodations for 100 guests were provided. There was a kitchen, storage buildings, dining hall, offices, and a church. All were built by Springer and his co-workers.

There was also a studio where Dr. Springer recorded messages that were broadcast on radio stations throughout the United States and, in fact, many foreign countries. His mail-order health food business grew. Increasing numbers of people were attracted to the resort.

Dr. Springer had a considerable impact on the neighboring town of Baker. He was the town's best single, commercial customer, and he could be counted on as a main participant in any community enterprise. On the basis of his volume of mail, Baker acquired a first class post office. Frequently the motels in Baker accommodated people waiting to get into Zzyzx.

An interesting feature of the construction and maintenance of Zzyzx is that most of the work was done with men recruited from Los Angeles' missions. Dr. Springer brought them to Zzyzx -- they helped construct the buildings, they maintained the grounds in immaculate condition, and all the while efforts were made to help them reconstruct their lives. They were paid a small wage called a "helping hand." Thus, more than 4,000 men were given a new chance at Zzyzx. Many went back to the missions; but many others were rehabilitated and returned to their loved ones and useful lives.

The atmosphere that Springer created and maintained at Zzyzx was one of peace and Christian charity. Alcohol was not permitted on the premises at all, for either guests or workers. If guests were observed with alcohol, they were asked to leave. Smoking was not permitted, although this was not enforced as rigidly as alcohol use. Drugs were not even thought of. Arguing was not allowed, but constructive debate was encouraged. Children were welcome. Abundant quantities of good healthy foods were served. If people were unable to pay, they could stay at Zzyzx without charge.

The atmosphere was constructed to optimize the chances that people who needed a lift and were perhaps suffering from ailments more caused by psychological dispositions than germs, could come, relax and get sunshine, eat good foods, and improve their condition. It worked admirably well for literally hundreds of thousands of guests over the years. But as the decade of the 1960s commenced, and the Springers entered their 17th year at Zzyzx, there was a cloud on the horizon. The government became determined to expel the Springers from Zzyzx.

Throughout the 17 years the Springers had continued to operate on the basis of their mining claims. Of course, they were interested in perfecting their claim to the land and gaining patent. On an average of once every three months for those 17 years, they had visited the U. S. Land Offices (BLM) in Los Angeles, Riverside, and Sacramento. They had kept officials fully apprised of their actions and progress and until about 1961, they had no indication anything vital was wrong.

In 1968 BLM commenced legal action against the Springers to evict them from the land at Zzyzx. By then they had been living there and improving the site for 24 years. We may never know what motivated the government to do this. Almost simultaneously, charges were brought against the Springers by the Internal Revenue Service for alleged evasion of federal income tax payments and by the California State Food and Drug Commission on a variety of charges dealing with their line of health foods.

Why did it happen? In 1974 an article in the LOS ANGELES TIMES makes the claim that it was an article that appeared in their paper in 1967 that precipitated the actions against Springer. When you first read that article, it doesn't seem the points made in it could have moved three government agencies (and perhaps more) to take action against the Springers. But if you read it more closely, it can be seen the article suggests that the Springers were "trespassers" on government land and probably owed the government rent; that they sold health foods of questionable value; and that they did not properly or completely discharge their income tax obligations. And when you consider the awesome influence of the TIMES, then it begins to seem more likely. It may be possible the TIMES is correct; that it was their article in 1967 that was the catalyst in motivating

175.

101.1 these government agencies to move simultaneously against the Springers in 1968.

BLM officials are generally reluctant to discuss the subject of Zzyzx. One high-ranking official objected to the language used in the preceding paragraph. He stated that BLM had been investigating and pursuing a trespass case against the Springers for some years before 1968 (which seems likely) and that the TIMES article played no role in motivating BLM to take action. He did state, however, that he felt the TIMES article could well have been a factor with the other agencies.

In the initial action, more than 60 charges were brought against Dr. Springer by the California State Food and Drug Commission. In response to what might have been poor advice from a lawyer, Springer pleaded guilty to several charges of making "false and misleading statements" about certain of his products. Apparently these were seen by him as being mere technicalities having to do mostly with requirements for certain of the labels he had used for many years to be updated to be in compliance with new rules. These charges did not deal with the quality of the health foods in a substantive way. The state dropped the rest of the charges which numbered more than fifty.

More than seven years after the Internal Revenue Service had brought charges of income tax evasion, Dr. & Mrs. Springer were acquitted of all charges in June of 1977.

But the most serious of the actions brought against them, and the one with the most far-reaching effects (leading directly to the present condition whereby we cannot now go to Zzyzx without first requesting special permission) was the trespass and eviction action brought by BLM. BLM stuck with the case tenaciously on the ground that the Springers had misused mining claims.

On April 11, 1974 (Good Friday), after spending nearly 30 years there, Dr. and Mrs. Springer were bodily evicted from Zzyzx. They had 36 hours to remove their personal property accumulated over a period of 30 years. They were threatened with handcuffs and escorted off the property by armed deputies. Zzyzx was returned to the public domain under custody of the victor -- the Bureau of Land Management.

Suddenly BLM had a white elephant on their hands. They had never known all those years as they pursued the case against Springer what use they might make of Zzyzx should they be successful. And now they

176.

had won. They had no budget to take care of Zzyzx. The rats and cockroaches moved in; and even worse, even though caretakers were on the site at least part of the time, vandals began to destroy the buildings and other property.

Throughout 1974 and 1975, BLM's Zzyzx policy was beginning to appear in an increasingly unfavorable light. By late 1975, apparently pursuing a course of desperation, BLM decided that what they really wanted all along for Zzyzx was to return it to the condition it was in before Springer came there. "Push the buildings into the lake" became the watchword. Local BLM officials in southern California are quick to point out that the direction to "return Soda Springs to the condition it was in before Springer came there" emanated from headquarters in Washington, D.C.

At about that time, a group of colleges and universities from the California State system began to express interest in making use of the site as some kind of studies center. The "destroy the buildings" orders were held in abeyance as negotiations were made and possibilities explored. It was thought something could be worked out whereby this group of schools -- later called the "Consortium" -- would share the expense of operating Zzyzx with BLM. BLM rethought its position. They didn't want to push the buildings into the lake after all! What they really wanted all along was a desert studies center!

It is interesting and important to note that at this same time the public was clamoring to gain some kind of interest for themselves at Zzyzx, some kind of claim on its future use. For example, the California Association of Four Wheel Drive Clubs wrote letters of inquiry several times suggesting the site might be made use of as a headquarters for recreational activities. Also a group of 26 Y.M.C.A.s had a valid application on file for use of the site that had been pending since 1966. Ignoring these requests, BLM went ahead with plans for a studies center.

The public has complained about this ever since, but to little avail. In response to this pressure, in 1983 BLM initiated preparation of a management plan for Soda Springs or Zzyzx which effectively disfranchised the public entirely and virtually turned this resource over to the "Consortium." The Consortium has no interest in serving the general public and hence we are effectively closed out. BLM has asked that we include the statement "The public was involved in the preparation of

101.1   this plan (the Soda Springs Management Plan)."
Certainly there was an opportunity for public input but
any objective analyst or observer would conclude that
was merely a formality.

Time has shown that Zzyzx is a good place for
educational purposes. It has also shown that the general public -- especially those interested in the desert --
is fascinated by the Zzyzx site, and that it is a wonderful place for them to gather and have a positive
experience about the desert. Time has also shown what
should have been obvious in the first place: that Zzyzx
is not a good place for detailed basic scientific
research, because there is not much there that could be
considered natural habitat.

The image of Dr. Springer is an omnipresent thing
at Zzyzx. Those who come to Zzyzx get interested in
Springer and his story. The name Zzyzx is here to
stay, the spirit that the Springers brought to this
place will be present for all time to come.

As a sort of sop to the demands of the public,
BLM offered some complicated mechanisms by which the
public (including Mojave Road travelers) can gain
limited and brief access to Zzyzx. The following three
paragraphs were submitted by them for inclusion in the
Guide. They are reproduced verbatim and without
further comment:

"The approved management plan reflects these
feelings. The goals of management at Soda Springs
include using the site for educating both students and
the general public about the desert and the specific
resources of the area including Zzyzx Mineral Springs,
improving and maintaining the chub habitat, improving
and maintaining the marsh habitat, maintaining the
cultural resource base, and retaining the visual integrity of the Zzyzx-era facilities."

"The public can use Soda Springs in four ways.
Groups may make use of the facilities at the Desert
Studies Center for educational purposes by contacting
the Desert Studies Consortium at (714) 773-2428. Public
tours are offered by the BLM every weekend except
during the summer months; special group tours can be
arranged by prior arrangement; and Soda Springs is
open to special events. You should contact the BLM at
(619) 256-3591 to find out when public tours and special
events are being offered and to make arrangements for
special group tours."

"The BLM is seeking additional funding to have an
orientation center at Soda Springs and to provide for

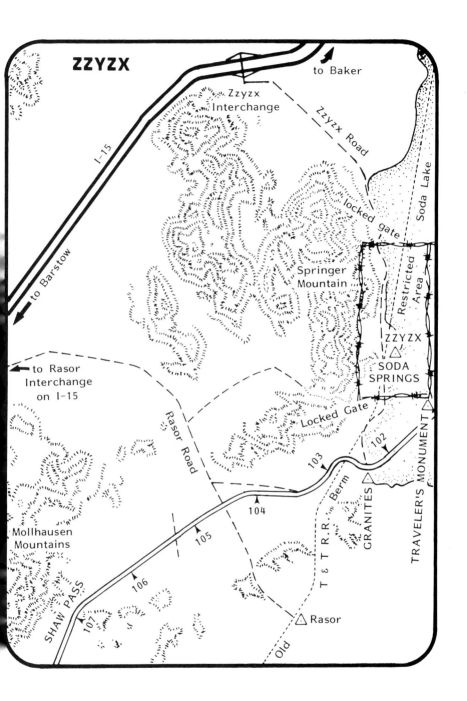

ZZYZX

to Baker

Zzyzx
Interchange

Zzyzx Road

I-15

locked gate

Soda Lake

to Barstow

Springer
Mountain

Restricted
Area

ZZYZX

SODA
SPRINGS

to Rasor
Interchange
on I-15

Rasor Road

Locked Gate

102

103

GRANITES

TRAVELER'S MONUMENT

104

T & T R.R. Berm

Mollhausen
Mountains

105

106

Rasor

107

SHAW PASS

Old

179.

THE GRANITES

A group of the Friends of the Mojave Road gathered at the Granites at Mile 102.4 preparing for a day's work on the Mojave Road Recreation Trail. December 31, 1981.

Paul Lord Photo

MOJAVE ROAD NEAR THE GRANITES
February 22, 1986
Dennis Casebier Photo

181.

101.1   public use on a daily basis. If you would like to volunteer your time to assist the BLM in managing Soda Springs, they would be glad to hear from you."

        BLM has urged us not to use the name "Zzyzx" for this spot, but rather to use "Soda Springs" almost exclusively. Their rationale is that Soda Springs is the older name. Their motivation is that they're trying to erase the memory of Dr. Springer and the great work he did at Zzyzx. Except for historical contexts, where you would automatically use either name depending upon the specific references, we lean toward Zzyzx. It was known by that name to hundreds of thousands of people who stayed there and by literally millions who heard Dr. Springer's broadcasts in every state in the United States and in many foreign countries. (1.3).

102.4   You are across the lake and at the Granites. This name refers to the small granite outcrops that occur here. It is quite a pretty spot on the southwestern edge of Soda Lake. There is a small spring -- a seep really. In the past it had a greater flow than it has now. It could be developed to make water available for wildlife and limited vegetation. If developed carefully over the years, it could become a sort of poor man's Soda Springs for travelers on the Mojave Road and would give a bit of a taste of what Soda Springs is like and how it might have appeared to travelers on the trail. There are nice camping spots in and around the Granites, and of course, this site is immediately adjacent to the open off-road vehicle area to the south. (0.0+).

102.4+   As you leave the Granites, there are several ways you might be drawn off in the wrong direction. We've put out sufficient cairns so if you'll take the time to spot the next one ahead before moving on, you'll probably have no trouble. Initially, leave the seep and head northwest toward Springer Mountain and pick up the cairns on the trail. (0.3).

102.7   The route of the Mojave Road passes over the abandoned grade of the old Tonopah & Tidewater Railroad, but it does not follow it. The T&T was the child of Francis Marion Smith, also known as "Borax Smith." The principal motivation for its construction was to service his "Lila C" Borax mine in the Death Valley country. As it worked out, the T&T outlived the Lila C by a large margin, and it survived longer than most other desert country short lines. It had a really nostalgic charm about it; it was the "neighborhood railroad" for the people of the desert country. It was as unstructured, undisciplined, and unpredictable as the

02.7   desert people themselves. It's a shame it couldn't continue operating. We believe we'd be comfortable with it ourselves.

      The T&T never lived up to either element of its name, it never went to either Tonopah or Tidewater. (That is, it never reached the ocean. There is, however, a spot on the T&T near Broadwell Lake called "Tidewater," but it was the hope of reaching the ocean and not this spot that gave rise to the name of the railroad.) In August of 1905 construction commenced at Ludlow, a station on the Santa Fe 31.6 miles south of here. The line was pushed past here early in 1906, and reached the town of Silver Lake, 18.4 miles north, in March of that year. Silver Lake was an important town in this country in those days. Baker did not exist at that time. The closest siding to the north was Soda Springs (the present Zzyzx) at 1.7 miles. The closest siding or station to the south was Rasor, 2.2 miles distant. The T&T ultimately was extended to Death Valley Junction, Beatty, and Goldfield.

      The T&T was not a profitable railroad, but somehow it managed to hang on even through the Depression of the '30s, generally on the promise of some new prospect or enterprise in the desert. Throughout most of its existence, the offices and shops for the T&T were in Ludlow. Crucero, the Spanish word for crossing, is the point 6.0 miles south of here where the T&T crossed what is now the main line of the Union Pacific. In 1933 the section of track between Ludlow and Crucero was abandoned, and the offices and shops were moved to Death Valley Junction. The road was then only operated from Crucero north. The trackage between here and Crucero was badly damaged by the great flood of 1938. Still, the road was rebuilt and operated until June 14, 1940. The tracks remained in place until 1942, at which time the rails were requisitioned by the War Department. By July of 1943 the rails had been removed from Beatty to Ludlow. Many of the ties were taken up by desert people for use in corrals, fences, and buildings, but many were left in place and can still be seen. (0.2).

02.9   Heavy blow sand area. Sand drifts over the road to a considerable depth. It takes 4WD to navigate it. The stretch of sand is not long, but it is usually soft. (0.7).

03.6   Faint road angles off to the right. It will take you to Rasor Road, but it's best to continue on straight to Rasor Road. In any case, Mojave Road traffic continues

103.6   straight ahead. (0.9).

104.5   Cross Rasor Road. There are actually three main tracks to Rasor Road at this point. It has a tendency to become very badly washboarded, so at least twice in the past, people have blazed paralleling paths. You should approach the three intersections with Rasor Road slowly because the crossings are rather deeply grooved and often there is heavy traffic on Rasor Road. If you turn to the right here (northwest) you'll come to I-15 in 5.1 miles and there is a gas station at that offramp. The road left takes you to abandoned Rasor Ranch and the open off-highway vehicle area in that vicinity. The Mojave Road continues directly ahead. Within three miles you'll be coming to blow sand. Beyond that, conditions get quite bad on the way to Afton Canyon for another six miles. The Rasor Road point is the last place to bail out before reaching bad blow sand and other rough conditions.

SPRINGER MOUNTAIN SIDE TRIP

A side trip can be made that takes you up the west side of Springer Mountain. Those who persevere will end up on top of the mountain (requires hiking) with a magnificent view of Zzyzx and Soda Lake spread out before them. It will require two hours or more. A strenuous hike is required to climb the last seven or eight hundred feet of the mountain (that's the change in elevation -- the hike itself is probably closer to a mile). To get there turn right or northwest on Rasor road. After traveling 1.6 miles there will be hills and rocks immediately to the left (west) of the road. Go to the northernmost point of these rocks. Turn right (northeast) up the large wash. There are no roads or cairns here at the present time, but the wash is not particularly difficult to follow. Watch your mileage closely. The road heads directly into the mountains. After traveling 1.4 miles, you'll see a wash coming in from the southeast. Turn up that wash. It will become increasingly sandy as you proceed. When this wash begins to approach the mountains, drive out of the wash to the left (north), drive up to the base of the mountains, and then stop. This is where you must leave the vehicles; also leave anyone here who isn't in shape for a strenuous hike. Take water and food. Also take cameras and binoculars if you have them, for once on top of the mountain, you'll be in for a rare scenic treat. At the present time there are no cairns up the

MOJAVE ROAD WEST OF RASOR ROAD
A view looking east from about Mile 106.3 back toward Springer Mountains (left) and Soda Lake beyond the mountains. October 17, 1975.
Dennis Casebier Photo

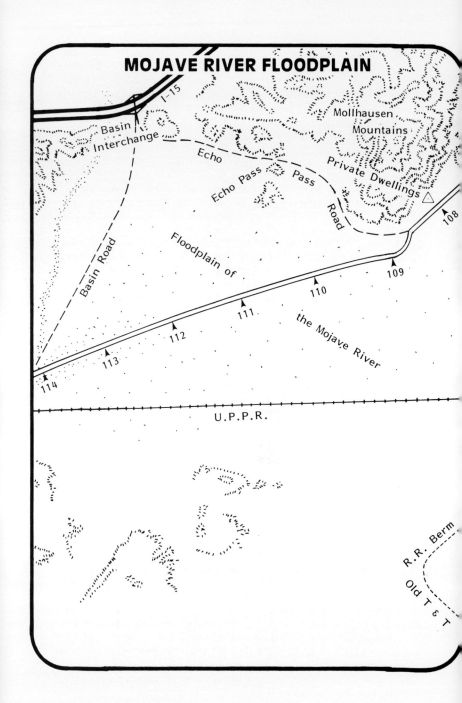

MOJAVE RIVER FLOODPLAIN

I-15

Mollhausen Mountains

Basin Interchange

Echo

Private Dwellings

Echo Pass

Pass

Road

108

Basin Road

Floodplain of

109

110

111

the Mojave River

112

113

114

U.P.R.R.

R.R. Berm

Old T & T

186.

4.5   side of the mountain. We plan to lay out the hiking trail and mark it, but that hasn't been done yet. You'll have to figure it out for yourself. It isn't terribly difficult. Proceed slowly and study the map. It will take a little more than an hour for people in good condition to hike to the top, look around a little while, and get back down. Once back down, return to Mile 104.5 on the Mojave Road and prepare to head west. (0.8).

5.3   Faint road crosses. Continue straight on well traveled road. (1.4).

6.7   We're entering a shallow pass named Shaw Pass, named in honor of Army Surgeon Dr. Merrill Eugene Shaw (see Mile 120.0 for a discussion of his fate on the Mojave Road). (0.2).

6.9   After you drop down from Shaw Pass, there is blow sand in the road. The road ahead features blow sand, loose soil, and all kinds of hazards to vehicles. It is inadvisable to venture beyond here without more than one vehicle. All vehicles should be properly equipped for back country travel. (0.9).

7.8   A driveway goes off to the right (north). There is private property here; there are several houses and outbuildings and the remains of a windmill. The area is occupied. As always along the Mojave Road, we should treat the inhabitants with the utmost respect and consideration. These buildings should not be approached under any circumstances, unless the owners invite you. Only with that kind of behavior, can we expect our own rights on the desert to be protected and respected by others. (0.3).

8.1   Remains of a windmill adjacent to the road on the right. Just beyond the windmill another driveway goes off to the right (north) to other buildings on private property. (0.3).

8.4   You are at a point of decision. The road you have been following and which appears to continue on ahead up out of the floodplain is called the Echo Pass Road. If you plan to follow the route of the Mojave Road directly across the floodplain to the mouth of Afton Canyon, then you must leave Echo Pass Road here (a little less than 0.3 miles beyond the remains of the windmill -- there are cairns showing the way), go to the left through blow sand, and drive down into the floodplain. If, however, you choose to bypass the rigors of the blow sand of the Floodplain of the Mojave River, then there is an alternate route. Referring to the detailed map, you'll see that if you continue on this road, you'll reach the Basin Road near I-15 in 4.6 miles. The only

108.4   obstacles on Echo Pass Road are a few places with bad
         blow sand (one particularly bad spot where sand has
         blown into a small wash) and a sharp little hill at Echo
         Pass. Once you arrive at Basin Road, you could
         continue along that road southward to the U.P.R.R. at
         the mouth of Afton Canyon, a distance of about 4.5
         miles.
              Assuming you have chosen the floodplain route,
         there is a problem of knowing where to head across this
         stretch. The way has been marked by placing
         thirty-odd railroad ties, telephone poles, and other
         structural timbers varying from 3 feet to 25 feet long
         on end in the sand, mostly within sight of each other.
         But they can get knocked down, or they might be
         hidden from view by vegetation and, consequently, you
         might lose that line of travel. It can therefore be
         essential that you stop here and survey the geography
         so you'll know where to head in case you lose the road.
              Straight to the west is a large dark mountain.
         That's Cave Mountain. Afton Canyon is at the left
         (southern) foot of Cave Mountain. Measured in degrees,
         the mouth of Afton Canyon is just a little under 20
         degrees to the left (south) of the main peak of Cave
         Mountain. If you study the area closely, you'll probably
         be able to spot it. Now for the good news. There's a
         limit to how far off the route you can get. Remember to
         steer to the left of Cave Mountain. The U.P.R.R. track
         is just a little more than two miles south of where
         you're standing. It heads directly toward the mouth of
         Afton Canyon, just as you are. Remember that you
         shouldn't drift so far south that you get close to the
         railroad until you're almost at the canyon. Another
         landmark to watch while crossing the floodplain is a
         strip of blow sand that stands out on the dark side of
         Cave Mountain about one-third of the way from the
         peak of the mountain to the mouth of Afton Canyon.
         When you get down into the floodplain you can always
         see that streak of sand. Head a little to the left of the
         sand streak, an angular amount approximately equal to
         the angle between the sand strip and the peak of Cave
         Mountain. This way you'll probably strike Basin Road a
         little to the north of the mouth of Afton Canyon. Simply
         turn left in that case on Basin Road and proceed until
         you come to the Mojave River, and then follow the river
         to the mouth of the canyon.
              The floodplain can be a fascinating place. The
         following description was provided by BLM: "The Mojave
         Floodplain is particularly beautiful in the spring when

ENTERING THE FLOODPLAIN OF THE MOJAVE RIVER
Picture taken from Mile 108.4 looking westward across
the Floodplain of the Mojave River toward the mouth of
Afton Canyon, which is just to the right of where the
antenna on the vehicle cuts the horizon. December 27,
1981.

Dennis Casebier Photo

IN THE FLOODPLAIN
Two Land Rovers take a noon break at a typical loca-
tion out in the Floodplain of the Mojave River. Cave
Mountain is visible on the horizon on the right side of
the picture. December 1, 1985.
Dennis Casebier Photo

FLOODING IN THE FLOODPLAIN

The Floodplain of the Mojave is so dry and dusty that most visitors wonder why it is called a floodplain. Once in a great while (certainly not every year) the Mojave River floods and as it comes out of the mouth of Afton Canyon it spreads out across the floodplain, as is shown in this picture. It can be extremely dangerous at these times and should be strictly avoided. The vehicle in this photo took a great risk. March 3, 1983.

Dennis Casebier Photo

GUIDE POLES ACROSS THE FLOODPLAIN
The Riverside Ruff Riders erecting guide poles across the Floodplain of the Mojave River. February 26, 1983.
Dennis Casebier Photo

3.4   the desert willows and other plants are blooming. When you get into the floodplain, stop your vehicle (on firm ground, of course), shut off the engine, and walk out into the sand. Fill up your senses with the buzzing of the bees, the flitting of the hummingbirds, and the fragrant bouquet of the desert willows." (0.9).

9.3   As you proceed into the floodplain you'll cut through what appears to be a large wash. That's one of the channels of the Mojave River. When the Mojave floods in this direction, that's where there'll be water. You'll have to leave that channel as it swings too far to the north. Continue now to follow the poles or wheel tracks across the floodplain toward the mouth of Afton Canyon. (4.7).

4.0   You should strike Basin Road about this mileage and be in the bed of the Mojave River. There may or may not be water in the river at this point. Frequently it sinks into the sand near here for the last time. Or you might have to travel several miles upriver before encountering water on the surface. Of course, in times of flood, water may be well out into or completely across the floodplain. In fact, in times of great floods, you'd need a boat to get across the floodplain! Continue up the bed of the Mojave River. It will be assumed in this Guide that there is an average or moderate amount of water on the surface in Afton Canyon, and consequently you'll be able to drive up the river bed throughout the entire length of the canyon. In actual practice, the amount of water in the canyon can vary tremendously, and at times it is impassable.

IMPORTANT NOTICE. As we go to press with this book, BLM is preparing a special management plan for Afton Canyon. It is not known when the plan will appear nor what its features will be. There is a chance the canyon will be closed during summer months requiring travelers on the Mojave Road to obtain a special permit to pass through. Check with BLM Barstow while planning your trip. (0.1).

4.1   The Afton Canyon area and the country above it in the direction of Camp Cady are fascinating from a geological point of view. The area includes important fault lines that have been active in recent years. The following description of the Manix Fault Zone was prepared by Geologist Steven C. Semken.

THE MANIX FAULT ZONE

"Between Basin Road (Mile 114.0) and Manix Wash

193.

THE MOJAVE RIVER
Shortly after crossing Basin Road (Mile 114) the Mojave River might be encountered on the surface for the first time. Sometimes and at some places in Afton Canyon heavy mud might be encountered.
Dennis Casebier Photo

4.1   (134.0), the channel of the Mojave River (and thus the Mojave Road) runs across or closely parallel to the Manix Fault Zone, an area cut by several interlaced, active faults running approximately east to west. Geologists describe the Manix Fault as being of the left-slip type, meaning that net movements along each fault are roughly sideways along a near-vertical plane, and that each side of the fault moves to the left with respect to the other side."

"In contrast, the familiar San Andreas Fault Zone is right-slip: the motion is again sideways but in the opposite direction. Significant faults cross the Mojave Road at several places, and the most visible exposures of these are at the west end of Afton Canyon (Mile 120.3) and just east of Manix Wash (Mile 134.0). The "sharp" appearance of the fault contacts in these localities is indicative of recent activity."

"Anyone who doubts the significance of all this should consider the events of April 10, 1947, when a segment of the Manix Fault near Manix Wash ruptured, producing an earthquake of Richter Scale magnitude 6.2 that was felt as far away as Los Angeles and western Arizona. Had this not been a sparsely-populated area, the damage undoubtedly would have been quite severe. Some local effects of the earthquake were reported by Caltech seismologists C. F. Richter and S. T. Martner in the July, 1947 bulletin of the Seismological Society of America:"

"Manix Service Station: First motion felt was vertical, followed after one or two seconds by horizontal movement. A loud roaring or explosive noise was heard. Occupants were thrown to their knees and to the floor. A piano moved south three feet. Much dust seen rising from hills to the southeast. Earth fills slumped, lowering the highway a few inches, at bridges 54-219 (one mile east of Manix) and 54-223 (north of Field)."

"Mr. Royse, section foreman living at Field, went into the hills to the south and, besides finding displaced rocks, saw many landslides. He was near Harvard on a handcar at the time of the main shock. The car moved noticeably but remained on the track. Power lines were set into rotary motion like a child's skipping rope. The Mojave River increased in visible flow just after the main shock."

"There were twenty-five or thirty slides from steep cuts on the west side of the railroad near Afton. Newspaper reports that a trestle in Afton Canyon had settled seem to have been unfounded; however, there was much sliding and lurching on embankments, and extensive repairs were made necessary." (0.6).

114.7   There are several ways to enter the mouth of Afton Canyon, either by making use of the bed of the Mojave River or by gaining access via the Basin Road, which has several paths as you approach the canyon. In the immediate vicinity of the U.P.R.R. tracks at the mouth of the canyon, there are several sidings and it is apparent there has been activity of different kinds here for many years. This point is known as Basin -- or earlier as Baxter. On the north side of the river at the mouth of the canyon, you'll notice rather extensive ruins of previous mining activity. Larry Vredenburgh, researcher and writer about mining history in the desert, has written the following account of this spot:

"Between 1914 and the early 1920s the Sugar Lime Rock Company leased land from Southern Pacific Company and the claims of D. F. and S. A. Baxter and A. W. Ballardie situated just north of Baxter siding. During this time they quarried and processed limestone for the production of sugar. Reflecting on the fact that there was a post office here from June 1914 until March 1919 and then from June 1923 until June 1926, it appears that there were two periods of activity. In 1914 there were 60 men employed here, and the Union Pacific Railroad (at that time the Los Angeles, San Pedro & Salt Lake R. R.) constructed two miles of track which crossed the Mojave River to the north side. Operations ceased prior to 1925 and almost all the machinery and equipment were hauled to a limestone deposit at Chubbuck near Danby Dry Lake. Adjacent to the limestone quarries, iron has been intermittently produced from 1913 until present for utilization in the manufacture of cement." (0.8).

115.5   Cross under the railroad bridge near the mouth of Afton Canyon (east end). The entire length of Afton Canyon from here to the "Caves" is a place of great natural beauty. We will provide no special detailed log or directions. There are no cairns, as there have been very few since entering the floodplain. Simply follow the riverbed to the BLM Campground at the head of Afton Canyon. Please be very careful of the unique river habitat in Afton Canyon. Travel on sandbars. Don't drive in the water except when absolutely necessary, and stay completely out of the vegetation. Afton Canyon is not an off-highway vehicle play area. (0.4).

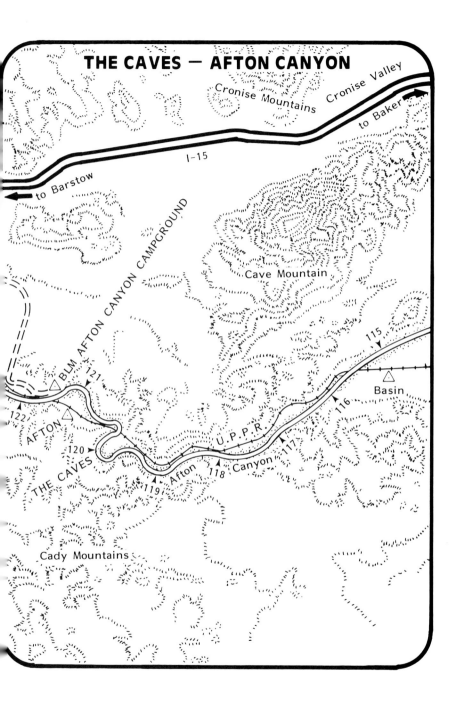

THE CAVES — AFTON CANYON

Cronise Mountains

Cronise Valley

to Baker

I-15

to Barstow

BLM AFTON CANYON CAMPGROUND

Cave Mountain

115

121

Basin

122

AFTON

116

U.P.R.R.

117

120

THE CAVES

Afton

118

Canyon

119

Cady Mountains

THE MOJAVE RIVER IN AFTON CANYON
A caravan of recreationists winds its way carefully through Afton Canyon crossing and recrossing the river many times. October 24, 1982.
Paul Lord Photo

THE CAVES

"The Caves" in Afton Canyon was the first stopping place on the Mojave Road west of Camp Cady. Sometimes the entrance is hidden by brush and trees, but if you search, you'll find it. Mile 120.2. February 12, 1967.

Dennis Casebier Photo

CARAVAN AT "THE CAVES" IN AFTON CANYON
December 29, 1981
Dennis Casebier Photo

15.9   The number of interesting side trips that can be made while traveling the Mojave Road is endless. The desert itself is limitless, you will be held back in enjoyment of it only by the bounds of your own imagination and curiosity, and in some cases energy and personal courage. Afton Canyon typifies the endless number of fun and instructive things to do in the desert. There is grand scenery everywhere so any hike is a thrill, no matter where started or how short. There are fascinating side canyons to explore. The presence of water attracts the full spectrum of Mojave Desert wildlife. In our use of Afton Canyon, we must be careful not to impact the scenic quality and we must be especially alert not to interfere with the wildlife. Be very gentle in your use of Afton Canyon. "Leave only footprints and take only photographs." (0.4).

16.3   The canyon walls have started to come together here and the real character of Afton Canyon begins to emerge. (1.0).

17.3   The southern wall of Afton Canyon in this vicinity is primarily grey and red conglomerate, a sedimentary rock composed of rounded particles of varying sizes, eroded from older rock beds. The grey conglomerate has itself been worn down to form the sharp pinnacles and tight ravines referred to as badlands topography. The material eroded from the canyon walls forms alluvial fans, the gentler, roughly triangular slopes extending from the ravines down to the river bed.

        Comments on geology by Steve Semken: "The steep-sided promontory extending from the north wall is also composed of conglomerate and alluvium. Behind it is a chaotic jumble of igneous and metamorphic rocks sliced by a network of small faults. Further north, not visible from the floor of the canyon, is Cave Mountain, a large mass of red granite (another Mesozoic pluton). The ravines leading up the north wall are treacherous, and should be attempted only be experienced desert climbers, but the view of Afton Canyon and the surrounding mountains from the rim is superb." (2.7).

20.0   You are at the Caves in Afton Canyon, just before you reach the middle railroad bridge, and on the left side of the canyon facing upstream. In the old days, this was the regular camping place on the road between Soda Springs and Camp Cady. These natural caves were more extensive in wagon road days. Now they are sometimes almost completely hidden by brush.

        In early historic times the stretch of road between the Caves and Marl Springs was the most dangerous.

120.0   The Indians lived in secret places in this seemingly barren part of the desert. They could watch the wagon road for great distances. Once in a while travelers would appear that offered tempting targets. That happened here at the Caves once, resulting in the killing of an Army officer.

On that day, October 16, 1867, the mail buggy was passing over the trail headed for Arizona. The reins were in the hands of Sam Button of San Bernardino. There was one passenger -- Dr. Merril E. Shaw, an Army surgeon. There was an escort of one soldier, Pvt. Timothy Donovan of Company "K" 14th Infantry from Camp Cady. The soldier was mounted on a mule.

The mail party stopped here at the Caves for lunch. Shortly after proceeding in the direction of Soda Springs, at a point not far from the Caves, the party was attacked without warning by 15 or 20 Indians. At the first fire, which was reported to be "half a dozen bullets and a dozen arrows, delivered at not more than 10 yards," Dr. Shaw was hit in the neck, and the escort's mule was struck in the shoulder.

Donovan abandoned the mule and jumped on the mail buggy. Button whipped his mules and headed for Soda Springs, some 15 miles distant, while Donovan cut the baggage loose, which included the mail and Shaw's trunk. The Indians chased the buggy on foot for some eight or ten miles.

Sam Button pushed the mail buggy on to Soda Springs as fast as he could. They arrived there late in the evening. As luck would have it, Capt. James P. Brownlow, 8th Cavalry, with a party consisting of approximately 150 recruits, mostly from companies of the 14th Infantry in Arizona, and the usual assortment of horses, team mules, and wagons, were encamped temporarily at Soda Springs.

Brownlow did not have the supplies or other equipment to permit him to take to the field after the Indians, but the presence of this large detachment put an end to any idea the Indians might have had to attack the station or further annoy the mail buggy.

Dr. Shaw was alive when the party arrived at Soda Springs, but he was mortally wounded. With Brownlow's help, he wrote a letter to his father in New York. He died the next day and was buried at Soda Springs. It is believed his remains are still there in an unmarked grave. A pass in the Mollhausen Mountains (Mile 106.7) is named for Shaw. (0.3).

202.

20.3 Reach and pass under the second or middle railroad bridge. Just beyond the bridge, a graded road leads off to the left. It will take you to the buildings at Afton railroad siding or to the BLM campground or you can continue along the river. If you continue along the river, you will encounter low riparian grasses and shrubs. Avoid this vegetation and the water whenever possible for they are the homes of numerous turtles and frogs.

Directly east of the point where the Mojave Road crosses beneath the middle railroad bridge and makes a sharp westward bend, part of the Manix Fault may be clearly seen in the wall of the canyon. The fault plane is visible as a sharp, nearly vertical discontinuity between the reddish Cave Mountain granite on the right and blue-grey metamorphic rocks on the left. The rock nearest to the fault contact has been fragmented (brecciated) and worn down by movement along the fault.

In Afton Canyon the vegetation can be quite dense; there are extensive growths of arrowweed and tamarisk, some smoke trees and rabbit brush. There appears to be two species of rabbit brush -- rubber and stick. (1.1).

21.4 At this point you have just passed the buildings that comprise the railroad maintenance station of Afton. A major graded road crosses the river here. To reach the BLM Afton Canyon Campground, take the road to the right for a few tenths of a mile. In case you're inter- ested in returning to civilization at this time, the good road continues on beyond the BLM campground another 3.6 miles to I-15. There is a service station at this offramp which offers the usual services including gaso- line. The BLM Campground here is the only improved campground to be found directly on the Mojave Road throughout the 138.8 miles of the recreation trail. There are improved camp sites with toilets, picnic tables, sunshades, etc. The site is heavily used. The presence of large numbers of motorcycles and other ORV's can be a disturbance to a person seeking a relaxed desert experience; but you don't have to get many miles away to gain relief.

At this point, you have an option you can take, and it can be an important one. The old Mojave Road continues up the Mojave River here (up past the rail- road bridge that's immediately up the river from where you're standing in the water now wondering what to do next). On above the bridge there are areas that tend

121.4   to be marshy. At times this route is completely impass-
         able because of water and mud, at other times you can
         go through with no trouble at all. In any event, there
         is a detour that takes you around the worst of the
         marshy part. For this detour, take the well-maintained
         road to the BLM Campground, continue on as though
         you were going to I-15 for another 0.7 miles where
         you'll see a fairly good road dropping suddenly off to
         the left. The point where it passes under the railroad
         tracks (a small bridge) is clearly visible from your
         road. So long as you thereafter stay toward the north
         (right) side of the riverbed, you won't have any trou-
         ble with the marshy spots, except when the river is in
         flood or when it has recently flooded. But some will
         want to stay in the riverbed, so off we go up the river
         toward the upper railroad bridge!

                    WARNING!! IMPORTANT NOTICE!!

              If you decide to proceed on in the direction of
         Camp Cady, please be advised that it is not possible to
         go all the way to that point because of fenced private
         land. You will need to leave the Mojave River at Mile
         134.0 (Manix Wash). Also be forewarned that the road
         beyond here can be rough and very soft and sandy. The
         condition of the road beyond this point can vary con-
         siderably depending upon how recently the river has
         flooded, how hot and dry it has been, and how windy
         it has been. There is no way here we can tell you how
         bad the soft sand is going to be. However, our experi-
         ence has been that it gets worse the farther west you
         go. Therefore, if you're having trouble in the first
         couple of miles you might want to give it up and return
         to Afton Canyon. Very frequently it is necessary to
         reduce tire pressure beyond this point if you haven't
         already done it. Another caution -- if the Mojave River
         is flooding (however low the stage) you should not
         proceed upriver from this point. (0.2).
121.6   Pass under the upper railroad bridge. The water is on
         the surface here and it can be quite muddy just beyond
         the bridge and for the first mile or more. Continue on
         close to the river itself, pick your way through the
         marshy-looking spots. Stay out of the vegetation as
         much as possible. Send one vehicle well in advance of
         the others, so only one gets stuck in case of bad mud.
              Geological comments by Steve Semken: "Fewer than
         one million years ago, the region from Afton Canyon
         westward almost to the Calico Mountains was covered by

TRIANGLES

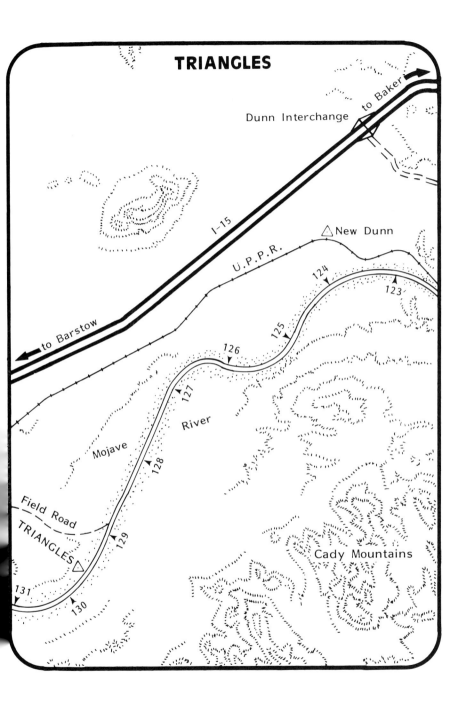

to Baker

Dunn Interchange

I-15

△ New Dunn

U.P.P.R.

124
123

125

to Barstow

126

127

River

Mojave

128

Field Road

TRIANGLES △

129

Cady Mountains

131

130

205.

121.6   a large lake, now referred to as Manix Lake. This lake
        was one of a chain of former and present-day intermit-
        tent lakes (the latter include Soda and Silver Lakes)
        that extended along the Mojave and Amargosa Rivers in
        a wetter period of southeastern California climate. The
        cutting of Afton Canyon by the Mojave River probably
        hastened the demise of Manix Lake. Today, the one-time
        bed of this lake is sporadically visible as a layer of
        light green sediments atop the badlands along the south
        bank of the Mojave, between the BLM Campground and
        the area south of Dunn Siding. Beach sands and grav-
        els may be found in the surrounding hills." (0.7).
122.3   To this point the railroad track has been close to the
        river on the right (north), but elevated about 40 feet.
        Also, there has been considerable marshiness with spots
        that could be impassable during wet periods. Beyond
        this point the railroad begins to move farther from the
        watercourse (to the right or north). You should angle
        to the right here to pass to the north of the water
        course and, in fact, completely to the north of the main
        mass of vegetation that's growing in the active river-
        bed. Once you leave the riverbed to avoid the mud,
        you'll find the surface to be increasingly sandy. Also,
        at this point you intersect the detour road mentioned at
        Mile 121.4. You can see where it passes under the small
        railroad bridge less than 0.1 miles away. (1.8)
124.1   The road (really it is just the river bottom) is quite
        sandy and can be really soft at times. The heavy
        growths of vegetation along the river are thinning out.
        Most of the trees are desert willows now whereas, a
        short distance below, they were mostly tamarisk. (0.4).
124.5   Dunn siding is visible off to your right at a distance of
        about 0.7 miles where the American Borate Company has
        had an active processing plant. (As we go to press
        with this edition of the Guide, we understand this plant
        is to be closed at least temporarily.) (0.8).
125.3   The left (south) bank of the river here is formed by a
        picturesque and barren group of hills that come right
        down to the river's edge. (1.4).
126.7   Those are the Cady Mountains to the south. In the
        riverbed, vegetation has thinned out considerably. Now
        there are only scattered desert willows. (1.9).
128.6   A fence line is visible on the right coming to the bank
        of the river. (0.3).
128.9   A fairly well-traveled road crosses the river here. We
        have put two cairns at the point where it reaches the
        main channel of the river. To the south this road takes
        you into the hills to mines that were worked many years

MOJAVE RIVER MILE 129.7
This is the point on the Mojave Road at which you turn
toward the north bank to visit the prehistoric ground
figures called "Triangles."   July 13, 1983.
Jim Brokaw Photo

THE TRIANGLES
A group of Mojave Road trekkers lined up beside one of
the Triangles. August 30, 1980.
George Bieber Photo

28.9   ago by Ken Wilhelm, but the mines are now inactive. To the north this road can take you back to civilization via Field siding on the U.P.R.R.

To go out by way of the Field Road, follow the road to the north up the wash and over a crest for 2.4 miles which will bring you to Field siding. The only problem is you're on the south side of the tracks, I-15 is on the north side of the tracks, and there is no grade crossing. To overcome this you can go either to the right or to the left. Do not try to cross the tracks. It is illegal and you could get hung up and hit by a train!

If you turn to the right, follow the frontage road that is displaced from the railroad tracks at a distance of 75 feet or so. Then in 1.1 miles you will have come to a deep wash (in fact, the 1.1 is measured down into the wash). There is a tunnel under the railroad at this point. It is small but will accommodate many 4WD vehicles (not trucks with campers). Pass through this tunnel. Proceed 0.6 miles to an intersection with a dirt road (well-traveled) and turn to the left. Then go 0.7 miles and you'll come to a well-traveled road heading directly toward I-15. Turn right on this road and follow it around a left-hand turn and in 0.5 miles you'll come to the Field onramp at I-15 and hence you can return to civilization.

If, however, you turned left instead of right back at the south side of Field siding, then in 5.1 miles along the frontage road (which again is displaced to the south of the railroad tracks by 75 feet or so) you come to Alvord Road at Manix. Turn to the right and cross the tracks. There is an overpass for Alvord Road to cross I-15 but there are no onramps. So, immediately on the north side of the railroad tracks (still south of I-15) turn left (west) on Yermo Road. In 3.0 miles you'll come to Harvard Road. Turn right (north) on Harvard Road and in 0.1 miles you'll come to I-15. (0.8).

29.7   You have arrived at a point opposite the prehistoric Indian site known as the Triangles. This spot where you're supposed to turn toward the right (north) bank is marked by a railroad tie buried on end in the ground and surrounded by stones, thereby forming quite a conspicuous cairn that is visible a considerable distance down the river. These intaglios, formed by prehistoric peoples unknown to us, were created by removing stones from desert pavement; all are in the form of triangles. They are up on a little mesa that borders the

209.

MOJAVE RIVER BED
At Mile 132.1 on the Mojave Road. The sand here can
be extremely dangerous when dry and the atmosphere
can be an inferno in this neighborhood in the summer.
December 1, 1985.

Dennis Casebier Photo

129.7   river. This particular mesa is a brown color on the
sides with a splotchy pattern of lighter colored material. If you look closely, you'll see the wooden (railroad
ties) posts of a barricade erected there many years ago
to prevent people who approach the site from above
from inadvertently driving on the intaglios. From our
position, if you want to visit the Triangles, you'll have
to turn toward the mesa here (turn right or toward the
north) and drive to the base of the mesa and then walk
to the top. The entire side trip takes about half an
hour. It is about 0.2 miles to the north to the base of
the mesa. Park and walk up the little crevice or ravine
that heads up to where the barricade posts can be
seen. It takes about ten minutes to hike up to the top
of the mesa -- up to the barricade mentioned before --
where the intaglios are, although care should be exercised in hiking up this steep slope over the loose
boulders. There are about 15 or 20 intaglios. The
largest ones are about ten feet long and about six feet
at the base. Please don't walk on the intaglios or
otherwise disturb the desert pavement at any point in
or near this fascinating site. You'll notice some damage
to this site. There are two sets of two parallel lines
each in the desert pavement that have been made in
recent years. These are helicopter tracks. Someone --
believed to be the military -- landed helicopters here
right on top of the intaglios and caused this damage.
No damage has ever been done at this site by ordinary
vehicles. (1.0).

30.7   You pass through an area that is fairly rocky. There's
a way around to the left (south), or you can grip the
wheel and drive over the rocks. The rocky stretch is
about 0.1 miles long. (1.4).

32.1   At this point cliffs about 40 feet high approach the
river on the left (southern) bank. You can drive right
up against them. It's a nice place for a break, and it is
a good landmark. The cliffs are of an earthen material.
At this point and beyond, the riverbed can be extremely soft and sandy. If you're having trouble, proceed
with caution. (0.3).

32.4   Geological comment by Steve Semken: "The Mojave Road
again crosses the Manix Fault Zone, and a fault contact
may be seen in the cliffs just north of this point. The
epicenter of the 1947 earthquake (discussed at Mile
114.1) was located north of the Mojave River near Manix
Wash, just a short distance from here." (1.4).

33.8   At this point, a fence line comes down to the river on
the right side. Apparently it crossed the river at one

211.

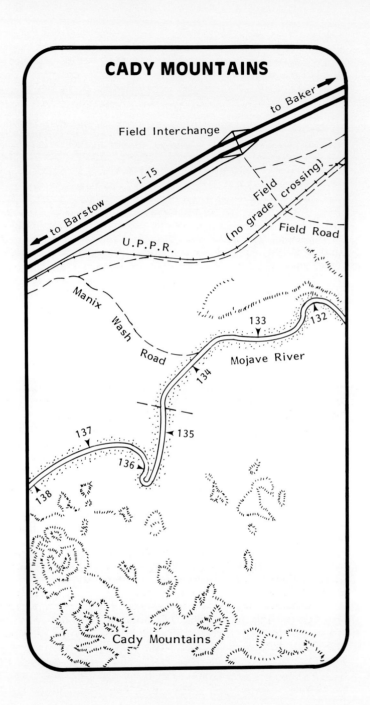

CADY MOUNTAINS

to Baker

Field Interchange

I-15

to Barstow

Field (no grade crossing)

Field Road

U.P.P.R.

Manix Wash Road

133

132

Mojave River

134

135

137

136

138

Cady Mountains

212.

133.8 time but it has been completely washed out in the riverbed. It is easy to spot on the north side of the river and it is an important landmark because it can help you find the entrance to Manix Wash -- the entrance to Manix Wash is on the right 0.2 miles beyond this fence line. Immediately bear to the right and head up Manix Wash as you must eventually exit here. (0.2).

134.0 This is an important wash to us because THIS IS THE LAST POINT WHERE YOU CAN LEAVE THE RIVER WITHOUT ENCOUNTERING PRIVATE LAND. If you continue on beyond here, you will run into a fence line that will prevent your passing on. So you must bail out here. Basically the formula is for you to find this wash and follow it up to the north till you're near (but not immediately adjacent to) the U.P.R.R. tracks, then turn left to Alvord where there is a grade crossing. Then you cross to the north side of the tracks and get on "Old 91," now called Yermo Road, and travel west to Harvard Road and hence on a short distance to I-15. Cairns are erected at the point where you should leave the Mojave River. The cairns occasionally get washed away by floods and the bank can be cut in such a way as to make the road difficult to see. You may have to hunt for it.

Following are directions for getting out of the Mojave River at Manix Wash: 0.2 miles from the fence line brings you to the edge of the Mojave River bottom. The banks pinch in and Manix Wash takes form as a shallow wash about 100 to 125 yards wide. Proceed up it. There are desert willows and mesquite trees in the wash. In another 0.3 miles a broad sandy wash comes in on the left. Stay to the right. There is interesting "badlands" topography off to the left. By the time you have gone 1.0 mile from the river, the Hoover Power Line comes into view. You'll be passing under that power line. This line was used in the 1930s to carry power to the Hoover Dam site while the dam was being constructed. It is now carrying power from the dam in the opposite direction. Just before you pass under the Hoover Power Line, there is an attractive-looking road going to the left that could draw you off -- don't take it -- continue on under the power line. You pass under the power line at a total distance of a little less than 1.5 miles from the river. At 0.5 miles beyond the power line, you intersect a good road that has been scraped. You can turn left on this road and reach Alvord Road and Manix in 1.5 miles. We have put a cairn on the northwest corner of this intersection, or you may

134.0   continue straight ahead here. After another 0.5 miles
         you'll be almost at the railroad and will intersect the
         same frontage road that is described in the directions
         for leaving the Mojave Road via Field at Mile 128.9.
         Turn left on this road and in 1.3 miles you'll come to
         the Alvord Road at Manix. In traveling along the rail-
         road, do not use the frontage road immediately adjacent
         to the tracks. There is a danger of being hit by heavy
         objects flying off high-speed trains. And there is no
         need for it because a second good frontage road is
         displaced a comfortable distance from the tracks.
              Turn right on Alvord Road and cross the tracks.
         You come immediately to the intersection of Alvord Road
         and Yermo Road ("Old 91"). Turn left on Yermo Road
         (there is no access to the freeway from Alvord Road).
         In 2.4 miles you pass Martha's Cafe on the right, where
         outstanding hamburgers and other delights for the
         inner man can be procured. The proprietress of this
         famous establishment is Martha Linden. She has operat-
         ed the cafe here for over 30 years. When the Interstate
         was built and robbed her of the highway trade, she
         stayed anyway and has a brisk local trade; plus a stop
         here has become a necessary element of the Mojave Road
         experience! Then 0.6 miles after (west) Martha's you
         come to the intersection with Harvard Road. Turn right
         on Harvard Road and in 0.1 miles you come to I-15
         where there are access ramps in both directions.
              At Manix (intersection between Alvord Road and
         Yermo Road) the point where the athel trees are drying
         up marks the site of Ken Wilhelm's home and service
         station. Ken and his family held forth here for many
         years, reaching back in time to when what is now I-15
         was only a dirt road and Ken's station at Manix was the
         last vestige of civilization you'd see when you were
         headed east. Ken -- recently deceased -- told about
         how they would watch the road to the east at night.
         Car lights would appear in the distance toward Cave
         Mountain. They would watch until the car lights quit
         moving and then they'd go pull the traveler out of the
         sand and into Manix. The station at Manix was more
         than a mere service station. Ken had the best machine
         shop in this part of the desert. Most kinds of repairs
         to those early vintage cars could be made right on the
         spot.
              Today the U. S. Army from Fort Irwin unloads
         tanks and other heavy equipment at the Manix siding.
         They then travel east between I-15 and Yermo Road to
         Manix Wash where there is room for them to pass under

134.0   I-15 and then continue north to Fort Irwin.
        If you wish, you can continue on up the river
        from this point (we are assuming you are back down in
        the Mojave River at the intersection with Manix Wash)
        but you will have to return eventually to get out via
        Manix Wash. (0.5)
134.5   A fence line comes down to the river on the north side
        at this point. It probably crossed the river at one time,
        but it has been washed out in the river bed. (0.2).
134.7   A road crosses here. (1.1).
135.8   There is a horseshoe bend in the river here. Water or
        mud is sometimes present at the southernmost point of
        the bend. There is a way to get up out of the mud flat
        onto the banks to the right and avoid the mud (some-
        times there is no mud at all). (1.7).
137.5   Someone always asks, "What happened to the Mojave
        Road in the 1880s? Why did it fall out of use? Why
        didn't it evolve into an interstate route like many other
        emigrant trails and wagon roads?" The answer is sim-
        ple. It has to do with railroad geography, and the
        requirements of railroad routes to follow easy grades.
        Wagons crossing desert country would climb steep
        mountains to get water. Availability of water was the
        limiting factor for teams with wagons. Railroad trains,
        on the other hand, would haul water great distances to
        avoid climbing mountains. As you have seen, the Mojave
        Road climbs through high and steep mountains. In 1868,
        the surveying party for the Union Pacific Railroad,
        Eastern Division, discovered that if you dropped 10 to
        20 miles to the south of the line of the Mojave Road for
        a railroad route, then the high mountains could be
        avoided. And that's exactly what was done. In the
        early 1880s when the Southern Pacific (now the main
        line of the Santa Fe) was built between Barstow and
        Needles, it was on a line displaced by about 20 miles to
        the south of the line of the Mojave Road. The Mojave
        Road was abandoned as a transdesert route in favor of
        the new railroad route, and that's why the old wagon
        road still exists out here in pristine condition today.
        Sections of the Mojave Road have continued to the
        present time to serve local needs. (0.6).
138.1   You may find a fence line here that marks the eastern
        boundary of the Ironwood Christian Academy property.
        We say may because this fence washes out when the
        Mojave River floods. There is private property beyond
        this point. If you do not have permission to pass
        through it, then it would not be proper to proceed in
        that direction whether there is a fence or not. (0.4).

THE MOJAVE ROAD AT CAMP CADY
The Mojave Road at a point near Old Camp Cady at
about Mile 138.8. July 13, 1983.
Jim Brokaw Photo

38.5   Intersect a fairly well-traveled north-south road. This
        road marks the eastern boundary of the Camp Cady
        Ranch. There are the remains of an old building here.
        The site of Camp Cady itself is ahead to the northwest
        about 0.5 miles or less through the underbrush. An
        access route from here has not been worked out. Spe-
        cific instructions for reaching the site of Camp Cady
        cannot be given. The Camp Cady Ranch is owned by
        the California State Department of Fish and Game. It is
        hoped they will work out a way that travelers on the
        Mojave Road can have an opportunity to visit this
        historic site. The prospects are not good. It would
        require cooperation between the BLM and the California
        Department of Fish and Game.
            To the north of here about 0.5 miles is the Iron-
        wood Christian Academy (or Ironwood Camp). If you
        plan to pass back to civilization by this direction, you'll
        need permission from the owners as the road is on their
        land. (0.3).

38.8   The Army Post of Camp Cady. Although you may or
        may not be able to visit the site of Camp Cady, some
        background and descriptive data about its history will
        be given here. Camp Cady, named for Maj. Albemarle
        Cady of the 6th U.S.Infantry, was first established on
        April 19, 1860, by Maj. James H. Carleton, 1st U. S.
        Dragoons, at one of the points along the Mojave River
        where the water flows on the surface most of the year,
        even in dry years. The camp was established at this
        important desert watering place to serve as an opera-
        tions point while Carleton's two companies of dragoons
        scoured the desert searching for Indians who had
        committed several murders. At the end of his campaign,
        he abandoned the post on July 3, 1860.
            The spot was a good one. The camp was reestab-
        lished by the California Volunteers on April 23, 1865. It
        was abandoned a second time on April 1, 1866. Howev-
        er, because of Indian depredations that occurred at
        about that time, it was reestablished the next month
        and then manned until 1871, at which time it was aban-
        doned permanently by the military.
            During those years it occupied two different sites
        distant from one another by about 0.5 miles. There are
        few remains at either site; you've got to know where to
        look even to see foundations.

                            END

                Hope You Had a Nice Trip!

CAMP CADY 1863 OR 1864
A view of "Old Camp Cady" taken by photographer
Rudolph d'Heureuse in 1863 or 1864.
University of California, Berkeley
The Bancroft Library

CAMP CADY 1972
A shot taken at Old Camp Cady October 7, 1972 for
comparison with the d'Heureuse photo of 1863 or 1864.
Dennis Casebier Photo

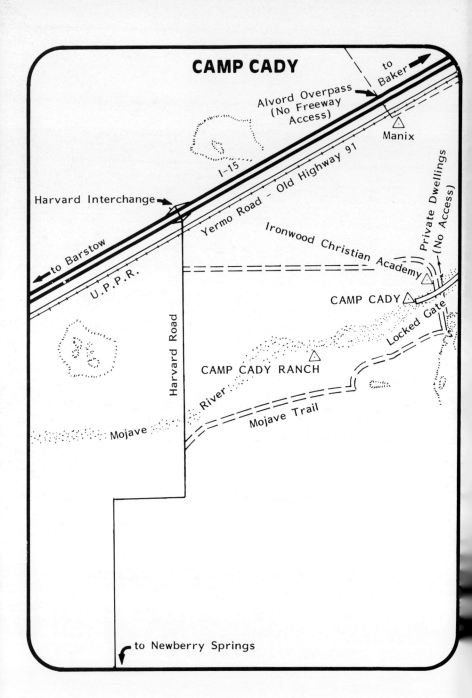

CAMP CADY

to Baker

Alvord Overpass
(No Freeway Access)

Manix

I-15

Yermo Road - Old Highway 91

Harvard Interchange

Private Dwellings (No Access)

to Barstow

Ironwood Christian Academy

U.P.P.R.

CAMP CADY

Harvard Road

Locked Gate

CAMP CADY RANCH

River

Mojave

Mojave Trail

to Newberry Springs

CARAVAN ON THE MOJAVE ROAD
About Mile 76
February 23, 1986
Dennis Casebier Photo

221.

MARTHA'S CAFE
This is "the place" to get a hamburger after completing
your tour of the Mojave road. It is on Yermo Road on
the north side of the road about a mile east of Harvard
Road. December 1, 1985.
Dennis Casebier Photo

MARTHA LINDEN
The proprietress of famous "Martha's Cafe" on Yermo
Road or "Old 91" just beyond the end of the Mojave
Road Recreation Trail. December 1, 1985.
Dennis Casebier Photo

AT NIGHT ON THE MOJAVE ROAD
A night picture taken at about Mile 63.8 on December 5, 1982.

Jim Brokaw Photo

THE MOJAVE ROAD AT NIGHT

by Spence Murray

On the extremely cold and windy night of December 4, 1982, Dennis Casebier and I in a Mitsubishi 4X4 truck equipped with auxiliary off-road lighting, and Jim Browkaw with wife Ann in a Chevy LUV 4X4, also with special lights, commenced a night run over the Mojave Road westward from Beale's Crossing at Mile 0.0 to the BLM Campground at Mile 121.4. The purpose was to check for visible lights with regard to points of access to the trail; not just for what it would look like (no sensible person should attempt the trail after dark) but to identify potential bail-out points in the event campers along the Mojave Road had a sudden emergency or other situation which would cause them to break camp at night. This was the return leg of the first-ever, single-day round trip of the Mojave Road. We also thought it might prove interesting to log the wildlife, nocturnal or otherwise, which we caught in the powerful auxiliary light beams.

The trip began at 7:45 p.m. in utter blackness at Mile 0.0. Driving without daylight was eerie. Our beams formed a tunnel of light ahead and the shadows cast by surface undulations and rocks actually made driving easier than in the daytime, but we soon became somewhat disoriented since there was no side-lighting to pick out familiar landmarks. Traffic lights moving along the road that runs between Needles and Davis Dam became visible, and quite high above us, at Mile 0.5 and remained so until we crossed that road at Mile 3.0. It was totally dark ahead though lighting from the settlements along the Colorado River were visible behind us.

Our beams made the cairns fairly prominent, especially those with a post, a length of pipe, or other reflective object in them. Traffic lights ahead and off to the right (north) came into sight at Mile 12.3 moving along U. S. Highway 95 which is crossed at Mile 14.3. A single light off to the right also became visible at Mile 13.3 which is a sometimes-occupied private residence near the road and which could be an important point of reference in an emergency. A side road to the house goes right at Mile 13.7.

There are no lights ahead after crossing U. S. 95 and starting across Piute Valley until Mile 17.9 when a cluster of lights becomes visible far to the right. This

225.

is the Coast Guard transmitter several miles to the north near U. S. 95. At Mile 20.4 the distant lights of Searchlight, Nevada, come into view off to the right.

No lights at all are in view on the detour around Piute Hill via the Cable Road until Mile 31.4 when the glow of lights from Las Vegas can be seen reflecting in the sky. A faint, single light appears just right of dead ahead at Mile 33.8 and which marks the headquarters of the OX Cattle Company Ranch on the Ivanpah-Goffs Road which is intersected at Mile 41.9.

West from here there are no lights until Kelso appears in the left distance at Mile 59.4, at the intersection with the Death Valley Mine Road, and where a single light at Cima also becomes visible to the right. The Kelso-Cima Road is reached at Mile 62.6. Beyond this intersection there is only blackness ahead but the Kelso lights intermittently disappear and reappear to the left as you move through an area where the Beale Mountains temporarily blank them, until they disappear completely from view at Mile 70 near Marl Springs.

The green and red lights of a micro-wave station on I-15 are visible to the right at Mile 74 and beyond. Traffic lights on I-15 will begin appearing intermittently at this point as well. The micro-wave station appears on and off to the right down through Willow Wash and vehicle lights moving along Kelbaker Road (which is not heavily traveled) may appear approaching the crossing at Mile 85.8.

At Mile 88.0, Seventeenmile Point, lights along I-15 and at Baker appear on the right a considerable distance away and will remain in view until Mile 102.4 at the Granites, but with no other lights ahead or off to the left. Beyond here, there are no lights in any direction along the Mojave Road, over Shaw Pass, to the Windmill at Mile 108.1, through the floodplain, and on to the mouth of Afton Canyon at about Mile 115.5, or into the BLM Campground at Mile 121.4 -- unless you happen to see a train with its bright light proceeding along the U.P.R.R. tracks.

The Brokaws bailed-out at Rasor Road at Mile 96.9 on our trip, while Casebier and I proceeded ahead alone. This is NOT recommended in a single vehicle in daylight, much less in the dark. We reached the BLM Campground dead tired but safely at 5:45 a.m. when it is still dark that time of year.

Wildlife encountered was at least equal to that seen on a daytime trip: 13 jackrabbits, seven small birds, three huge owls, and three kangaroo rats.

INDEX

227.

Other Books

by

Dennis G. Casebier

Camp El Dorado, Arizona Territory

Carleton's Pah-Ute Campaign

The Battle at Camp Cady

Camp Rock Spring, California

Fort Pah Ute California

The Mojave Road

The Mojave Road in Newspapers

Camp Beale's Springs & the Hualpai Indians

Nissan on the Mojave Road

Reopening the Mojave Road

Guide to the Mojave Road

Other Books Published by
Tales of the Mojave Road

A Sentimental Venture
by E. I. Edwards

Day After Day
by Jessie M. Frost

Maruba
by Maud Morrow Sharp

Send for list of books available to:
Tales of the Mojave Road
P. O. Box 307
Norco, California 91760

(714) 737-3150